Praise for

Get Empowered

"*Get Empowered* is a resource every person needs to walk through the world with their head held high and their dignity intact. We have all been impacted by sexual violence—whether it is our lived experience or it happened to someone we love. But that means we all need the knowledge and skills to face these experiences, so we have self-agency and can affirm our own dignity for ourselves and in our relationships. *Get Empowered* gives you all of these tools with compassion, strength, and courage."

—Rosalind Wiseman, author of *Queen Bees and Wannabes* and coauthor of *Courageous Discomfort*

"Read *Get Empowered* and you will feel safer and less lonely. This book speaks the truths we all need to hear. And most importantly, Nadia and Lauren will help you feel thoroughly supported in your journey to survive our disempowering world."

—Jeffrey Marsh, LGBTQIA+ activist and author of *How to Be You* and *Take Your Own Advice*

"*Get Empowered* is an inspiring, grounding, practical guide to securing our own freedom, and that of our communities. This book will help you name the life you want to live and to reckon with your inner obstacles so that you can also resist the outer obstacles. I wish I'd had this book to grow up with, but reading it makes me think it's never too late to own my power."

—Rinku Sen, racial justice strategist and writer

"An empowerment guide that should be on the shelves of every survivor—filled with messages to return to over and over again and share with loved ones. As a Black queer woman, I found *Get Empowered* an affirming tool for resistance and resilience, with holistic strategies that honor grace and compassion for the healing journey of all survivors. Reading this was a balanced praxis of trusting my intuition as a superpower and a gentle reminder that I am worthy of defending."

—Jewel Cadet, queer Black activist, entertainer, and speaker

"*Get Empowered* is a must-read for anyone who wants to overcome their fears, become empowered, and heal. A particularly powerful aspect of the book is its emphasis on caring for one's mind, body, heart, and spirit while doing the work of healing and growing. As I reflect on my life as a young woman, I wish that I would have had access to such a wonderful tool."

—Carmen Gelman, award-winning activist

"*Get Empowered* is critical reading for every gender-oppressed person. I grew up feminist and highly aware of sexism and gender roles intellectually, but it was the exercises in this book that helped me learn—and begin to unlearn—exactly how much I had internalized those roles. This book puts theory into practice in a transformative way."

—Autumn Whitefield-Madrano, author of *Face Value: The Hidden Ways Beauty Shapes Women's Lives*

GET

EMPOWERED

*A Practical Guide to Thrive,
Heal, and Embrace Your Confidence
in a Sexist World*

**NADIA TELSEY AND
LAUREN R. TAYLOR**

Illustrations by Nadia Fisher

A TarcherPerigee Book

An imprint of Penguin Random House LLC
penguinrandomhouse.com

Most TarcherPerigee books are available at special quantity discounts for bulk purchase for sales promotions, premiums, fund-raising, and educational needs. Special books or book excerpts also can be created to fit specific needs. For details, write SpecialMarkets@penguinrandomhouse.com.

LIBRARY OF CONGRESS CATALOGING-IN-PUBLICATION DATA
has been applied for.
ISBN 9780593539200 (trade paperback)
ISBN 9780593718698 (ebook)

Printed in the United States of America
1st Printing

Book design by Shannon Nicole Plunkett

To missing and murdered Indigenous women—and all whose experiences and existence are rendered invisible. —Nadia

———————————————————

To everyone who's been through something. —Lauren

CONTENTS

"BOUNDARIES ARE THE DISTANCE AT WHICH I CAN LOVE YOU AND ME SIMULTANEOUSLY."

—Prentis Hemphill

WELCOME

GROUNDING & CENTERING: A safe place. Think of a place where you can feel safe, whether it's real or in your imagination. Settle yourself into the safe place, taking a few conscious breaths. Ask yourself: What does it feel, smell, sound, and look like there? What's the temperature? Is anyone else—human or spirit or animal—there with you? Using all your senses, fill in as much detail as you like. When you're ready, transition back to the present moment by focusing again on your breathing. You can go back to this safe place whenever it's helpful.

Welcome to *Get Empowered*, a book about protecting ourselves, including our inner selves, from the effects of gender-based harassment, abuse, and assault. We're cheering you on for setting out on a journey that we, Nadia and Lauren, have taken to reduce the barriers that can make speaking up difficult, to gain skills for self-protection, and to create bigger, more authentic lives (and let's be real: it's an ongoing process, and it's not always simple).

Gender-based violence restricts our lives and causes us harm. Whether or not we've experienced it directly, we're all affected by the fact that we live in a world where all

Gender-based violence is harm done based on actual or perceived gender, sex, sexual orientation, or gender expression. It's a manifestation and reinforcement of unequal power relationships among genders and sexual orientations. It most commonly shows up as sexual violence (including sexual harassment), partner abuse, stalking, and sex trafficking. (For more, see the spectrum in Chapter 2.)

forms of gender-based violence and rape culture are so widespread. They harm us emotionally, mentally, spiritually, financially, and often physically.

For those of us who are the targets of gender-based violence, social and cultural forces rob us of our natural skills for self-protection and train most of us to be passive, scared, and compliant. This makes us vulnerable to harassment, abuse, and assault.

Rape culture is a culture in which sexual violence is pervasive and treated as normal, and victims are blamed for the assaults against them. It's not just about sexual violence itself but about cultural norms and institutions that protect those who rape, shame victims, and demand that women be responsible for avoiding sexual violence. The norms include things like victim-blaming, slut-shaming, sexual objectification, trivializing rape, denying how widespread sexual violence is, and refusing to acknowledge the harm it causes.

Get Empowered is about the ways you can:

- Defy the messages telling you to be small or passive
- Challenge shame and blame
- Better understand your choices and behavior
- Gain skills to value and advocate for yourself
- Make choices that will help you get more of what you want and deserve
- Live your life feeling more safe, confident, and free.

TAKING CARE OF YOURSELF

Even though this book focuses on empowerment and on solutions to gender-based violence, you may sometimes find it upsetting to read and to complete the exercises because we're talking about hard topics and looking at hard experiences.

We encourage you to have a plan for taking care of yourself while you engage with the book (for more about self-care, see Chapter 1). We'll give you suggestions, including a grounding exercise at the beginning of each chapter and a reminder about self-care at the end.

Feel free to use the grounding exercises from the beginning of each chapter whenever you'd like help calming your nervous system or building your resilience.

And if you already have something that works for you—use it!

Consider trying a grounding and centering exercise every time you open this book, or every week. Experiment to find the ones that work for you. If

A **trigger** is anything that sets off a memory of a traumatic experience. It can be a noise, smell, temperature, other physical sensation, or visual image. When we're triggered, we're usually so filled up with feelings related to the old trauma that we're unable to focus on the present, and we can't think rationally or regulate our emotions like we usually can.

you find yourself anxious or stressed out or triggered while working through this text, check out the Resources starting on page 245.

We suggest you don't read or work with the book right before bedtime (in case it stirs up feelings—we want you to get your sleep!) and make sure you have people you can call and additional resources available (see "Build Your Crew" in Chapter 10).

Also, if you're living with someone who is abusing you, consider leaving the book with a trusted friend, leaving it in a sealed envelope, or putting it in a place that only you are likely to look.

WORKING WITH YOUR BREATH

One tool for staying calm and grounded is conscious breathing—we'll be mentioning it a lot! We know you're breathing all the time, but noticing your breath, focusing on the inhale and the exhale, or deliberately deepening your breath helps on a different level. (We'll talk more about this when we talk about fight, flight, and freeze and the nervous system in Chapter 8.) To help yourself remember to take a deep breath when you need it, you can practice throughout your days—whenever you're irritated or scared or upset. Keep breathing in mind as you read the exercises and stories in this book, starting now.

Nadia's Story
I couldn't find the words

Get Empowered is partly the result of a painful experience in which I didn't speak up for myself. It was a turning point that made me determined to make a change.

I went to a thrift store to buy a pair of jeans. There was no dressing room—just an aisle in the back where boxes were stacked.

While I was changing, an employee entered the area, and with his back to me he began sorting through the boxes. I was uncomfortable, but I didn't say anything because he was just doing his job and I didn't want to seem paranoid.

He then turned around and asked me how the jeans fit. I dismissed my feelings of discomfort and answered him. He then put a tape measure around my waist. Convincing myself that he was trying to help me—after all, jeans come in waist sizes—I said nothing but resolved to speak up if he "did anything." He then put the tape measure around my thigh. Again, I didn't say anything, telling myself he was trying to get me the best fit.

Finally, he pulled down the jeans and measured my naked thigh. At that point, I was out of excuses for him and out of denial: I was sure something was wrong and told him to leave. He did.

But it wasn't over: I left the store filled with self-hate.

I felt the whole assault was my fault for continuing to give him the benefit of the doubt. I didn't tell anyone what happened for a long time because I was sure no one else would have been as stupid as I had been.

I needed to understand where my passivity had come from. Eventually, I found that I wasn't the only one; many others would've acted as I had.

After I started training in martial arts and gained physical skills and confidence, I was able to deal with situations involving obvious harassment and even assault. But I still had trouble with unclear situations that called for trusting my intuition and taking action. Any time I wasn't positive I was in danger, or I didn't want to hurt someone's feelings or be seen as rude, my old reactions—and inaction—took control. I discovered that changing this mindset takes time—yet it's so worth it.

Bottom line: I wrote *Get Empowered* because I needed to hear—and learn—the things in it.

Lauren's Story
Out of touch with myself

Standing up for yourself involves knowing how you feel, knowing what you want, and being able to say it. I was stuck on the first: I was so out of touch with my emotions that I couldn't figure out how I felt about most things. Much of the time I felt sad. Occasionally I felt happy and could have named it, but I definitely couldn't identify shame, anger, guilt, hurt, pleasure, connection, contentment, or anxiety, even though I felt them.

I needed to find a way to identify and connect with my feelings, use that information to decide what I wanted, and then have the skills to say it out loud and to feel okay about speaking confidently! Three steps.

Taking empowerment self-defense classes (okay, along with therapy) is how I was able to make that change. The first and most transformative thing I learned was that *I do have power.* For the longest time, I believed there was nothing I could do if someone tried to attack me or otherwise cross my boundaries.

Empowerment self-defense teaches practical skills to those targeted for gender-based violence—primarily women and LGBTQIA+ people. The combination of verbal and physical skills works for avoiding, interrupting, responding to, and healing from the effects of interpersonal violence. It's what Nadia and Lauren teach and is the basis of *Get Empowered.* (Find out more in About Empowerment Self-Defense on page 237.)

The realization that I have power transformed my life. I also learned that I have the right to speak up. I had less fear, more confidence. I was less angry and prickly because it was now safe to be kind. I found my voice. I learned how to ask for what I wanted and to say "no" when I wanted to.

For example, I had a boss who mistreated me and the team I managed. He would denigrate our department in meetings, say we weren't meeting productivity goals (even though we were), and refuse to give raises to those who were underpaid. I confronted him with all the facts and set some excellent boundaries in a long memo. When the bullying didn't stop, I found another job. (He was shocked that I would leave!)

Even more difficult was dealing with the homophobia and heterosexism coming from my mother when I was in my twenties. Just a couple of examples: she didn't invite my partner to family gatherings even though she invited my siblings' partners, and she told me not to be "obvious" about being a lesbian. I told her that I needed a break from being in contact with her, and that for me to resume being in touch, she'd have to treat me and my partner respectfully, not like something she was ashamed of. I went no contact, and after about a year, we got back in touch and her behavior was better.

The transformation—to more confidence and less fear, to being able to speak up for myself—led me to teach empowerment self-defense, which focuses on not only physical moves but also verbal, emotional, and mental strategies for self-protection. I've been doing it for more than thirty-five years, and my students have shown me I was far from alone in my struggles.

I'm able to do all those things now—know how I feel, know what I want, and say it—and empowerment self-defense is a big part of how I got there.

THE PROBLEM: GENDER-BASED VIOLENCE

Many of us face threats and violence because of our gender. Gender-based violence is so common that we may not always notice it, but it affects our lives deeply and in many ways. It shows up in forms ranging from irritating to life-destroying.

Some people face even more violence because they're also targeted based on race, ethnicity, religion, class, age, size, sexual orientation, immigration status, disability, and more.

All of the ways people are marginalized and kept from engaging in personal and group power build on each other, and all of them need to be addressed.

These forms of violence limit options in every part of daily life: work, home, friends, family, health, fun . . . everything. They can keep people dependent and afraid, affect their choices, and erode their belief in themselves as powerful human beings who are worthy of living in safety and being treated with respect. People are often left with self-hate, shame, and self-blame.

Marginalized refers to people and groups who, based on some aspect of their identity, are oppressed, discriminated against, and excluded in the social, political, economic, educational, legal, and/or cultural realms.

Every form of violence, verbal and physical, from microaggressions to full-on attacks, can affect how we feel about ourselves without our even realizing it. The threat of violence has led almost all of us, consciously or unconsciously, to change the way we live our lives.

For example, when Lauren was twenty-six,

Microaggressions are common verbal, behavioral, or environmental slights, whether intentional or unintentional, that communicate hostile, derogatory, or negative attitudes toward stigmatized or culturally marginalized groups. They are manifestations of the dominant group's power and entitlement and can be a result of ignorance or malice.

she wanted to leave the roommate life and get her own apartment. She looked at many places in the part of town where she lived, which was close to friends and work, but didn't think she'd feel safe in any of them. She ended up moving miles away to find an apartment that worked for her. Decades later, she realized that the daily street harassment in her old neighborhood made her scared much of the time and affected where she felt safe living.

THE COMPLICATION: SOCIAL AND CULTURAL PROGRAMMING

Unfortunately, many of us have been taught to be victims in the face of violence—whether emotional or physical. We've been trained *not* to take action when we're targeted for harassment, abuse, or assault.

As a result, when we try to protect ourselves verbally or physically, we often come up against social and cultural programming that teaches that being nice, helpful, likable, and compliant is more important than our safety and well-being. It's layered with racial, ethnic, gender, and other cultural norms related to identity that affect the ways we react.

This training shows up in thoughts like these:

- "I'd say something, but I don't want to be rude or make a scene."

- "I don't want to hurt their feelings."

- "If I say something, they might make my life at work even harder."

- "If I stick up for myself, they might not like me."

- "What if I set a limit and it makes the situation worse?"

- "If I push back, they'll dismiss me as an 'angry Black woman.'"

- "What if they don't mean anything by it?"

- "I don't want people to think I'm a bitch."

- "If I don't let them help me, even though I don't need their help, they'll hold it against all disabled people."

And some of us have learned to become aggressive, to escalate, in the face of disrespect or boundary violations. But that doesn't necessarily keep us safe either.

These inner messages can stop us from speaking up for ourselves or taking action that could help us avoid danger. And they can get in the way of healing from whatever we've been through.

So even if we do know how to advocate for ourselves or set a limit, we can't always do it—and that fact can be extra painful. We end up likely to feel responsible and guilty for anything that *does* happen. So a cycle of self-blame (which others reinforce by victim-blaming) begins. And because most of us are reluctant to speak of experiences that cause us shame or for which we blame ourselves, silence around the violence continues.

> **Victim-blaming** is examining the victim's or survivor's behavior to explain why violence happened rather than looking at the harasser's, abuser's, or attacker's behavior. This may look like believing that violence happens because of what victims are wearing, how drunk they were, or because they didn't disclose that they're transgender.

HOW THIS BOOK CAN CHANGE YOUR LIFE

This book will help you dismantle your internal barriers to resisting, to speaking up, and to protecting yourself.

When you do the work in these pages, you'll be changing your own life—and be part of a movement to change the world. As a result, you'll be able to live a safer, more confident life.

Shifting our own behavior can be life changing:

- We can restore our instincts and build skills for taking care of ourselves and avoiding potentially dangerous situations.

- We can more easily tell people what's okay and what's not okay with us, and just as easily tell them what we want. This boosts confidence and our sense of personal power, even if we don't get what we hope for.

- We can shut down many assaults during their early phases, before they escalate.

- We can protect our hearts from verbal and emotional attacks.

- We can reduce the effects of trauma and heal from the harm we've experienced by gaining an understanding of what happened and releasing self-blame and shame.

- We can become active, confident, self-loving participants in the world, thus changing the ways violence affects us.

- We can become more creative and flexible, and we can have more strength and wisdom in our own lives and toward others.

- We can hold people who commit violence—and the society that condones it—accountable.

- We can become models of courage, respect, and healing.

- We can become advocates for larger-scale change.

- We can take up space in our own lives and live the lives we want.

We made those changes for ourselves and went on to teach others how to do the same. *Get Empowered* grows out of our experiences as women, empowerment self-defense teachers, martial artists, lesbian and queer people, and workers in a rape crisis center and in a shelter for abused women and their children. We want to share the possibility of transformation with you.

Ultimately, our goal is to help you live your fullest, most authentic life. We're so glad you're here!

The Self-Defense Paradox

You might be asking: Why should I have to do this? Why shouldn't those who are responsible for gender-based violence be responsible for ending it?

We say: good point!

We believe *all* the people using *all* the strategies are needed to create a safer, more respectful, and more inclusive world. Those of us targeted for gender-based violence (and for gender-based violence combined with racist, ableist, and other oppression-based violence) shouldn't have to sit around waiting for the world to change before we're safer and able to live bigger lives. We can act on our own behalf while we live in the world as it is now.

That's the self-defense paradox. We know aggressors are 100% responsible for the harassment, abuse, and assault they carry out. That's so important, we're going to say it again:

> *Aggressors alone are totally responsible for the harassment, abuse, and assault they carry out.*

Although people who are targeted can interrupt *some* harassment, abuse, and assault, the responsibility and blame belong entirely to the aggressors and to the society and culture that allow and facilitate their behavior. There's nothing anyone could do or not do that would make them deserve to be assaulted.

It's also true that those of us at risk of gender-based violence can take action to increase our own safety. Both these things are true at the same time: it's never our fault, *and* there are things we can do about it.

Doing this work won't guarantee you'll never be targeted, be treated disrespectfully, or have your boundaries crossed. We can't control harassment, abuse, or assault because we can't control those who do it.

But we can reduce the chances we'll be targeted. We can build our toolboxes for resisting. We can heal the harm we've experienced. We can ditch shame and self-blame. We can recognize who's really responsible and hold them accountable. We can claim our power, ourselves, and our lives.

HOW TO USE THIS BOOK

The best way to use *Get Empowered* is the way that works for you. You could start at the beginning and read every word and do every exercise. You could turn to the chapters that call to you and complete the exercises that feel relevant. Not everything in *Get Empowered* will apply to you. Concentrate on the parts that are the most helpful to you. See if you can find the place where you're challenging yourself but not stressing yourself or pushing too hard.

Simply reading the book may be enough. Completing the exercises will bring about greater inner strength, confidence, awareness, and change in your life. Since *Get Empowered* is for *you*, and since everyone has their own strengths and challenges, feel free to choose only the exercises you resonate with, or adapt them so they fit your own experiences and so you'll get the most out of them.

We'll often provide you a place to write your answers. But don't think that means you need to write! You can draw or doodle your response. You can tell a friend or record your thoughts on your phone. You can use a sketchpad or a journal. Any way you engage with the exercises is a good way.

You can work with *Get Empowered* alone, with a trusted friend, or in a group. Speaking with others and sharing our experiences, fears, strengths, and successes is a powerful tool for change and healing.

Also, be sure to check out our website—getempoweredbook.com—where you'll find lots of resources and bonus content.

For everyone, especially for those of us who have survived some kind of violation—like child abuse, child sexual abuse, abuse in a relationship, stalking, sexual assault, trafficking, or even "just" harassment—being in our bodies and feeling present there can be scary. We invite you to make a plan.

MAKE A PLAN. How will you take care of your mind, body, heart, and spirit while you do the work of healing and growing? Write some notes about how you'll get support while you work with *Get Empowered*.

While I'm working on this book, I'll (fill in whatever works for you below):

Get support from others by: _____

_____

Care for and nurture myself by: _____

_____

Remember to take breaks by: _____

_____

Encourage myself by: _____

_____

Remind myself to take long, slow breaths by: _____

_____

Other ideas: _____

_____

GENDER AND LANGUAGE

Gender-based violence affects everyone. We know that people of all genders can be targeted for harassment, abuse, and assault, and people of all genders can be aggressors. We also know that the gender binary—the belief that everyone is either male or female—is false.

Because of these facts, in this book we'll generally use gender-inclusive language, which means we'll refer to people in a way that doesn't signal what gender they are. And because men commit the vast majority of gender-based violence, and the vast majority of those targeted are women, children, and LGBTQIA+ people, we'll sometimes refer to aggressors as men and those being targeted as women, LGBTQIA+, or whatever combination is accurate. (Most aggressors are men, but most men are not aggressors.)

LGBTQIA+, two spirit, and non-binary are gender identities and sexual orientations. *L, G,* and *B* stand for *lesbian, gay,* and *bisexual. T* stands for *transgender,* meaning someone doesn't identify as the sex they were assigned at birth. *Q* can stand for *queer,* which many people use as an umbrella term for LGBTQIA+, or as a way of saying they don't belong in any of the categories or that they aren't straight. *Q* can also stand for *questioning,* which means someone feels they may not be straight or cisgender but isn't sure how they identify. *I,* or *intersex,* refers to someone with one or more innate sex characteristics, including genitals, internal reproductive organs, and chromosomes, that fall outside traditional concepts of male or female bodies. *A* stands for *asexual,* meaning someone who doesn't experience sexual attraction at all or experiences it only under certain circumstances, for example, after forming a strong emotional connection. *Two spirit* refers to a person who identifies as having both a masculine and a feminine spirit and is used by some Indigenous people to describe their sexual, gender, and/or spiritual identity. *Non-binary, genderqueer,* or *gender diverse* describes those who experience their gender as falling outside the binary gender categories of "male" and "female."

In doing this, we can be more respectful and inclusive of everyone gender-based violence affects, helping everyone lead safer lives and recover from harm, while still recognizing how it shows up in many people's lives.

A few notes:

- All the stories we use in *Get Empowered* are real. Some are compilations of more than one person's experience. Some have identifying details changed, including names; where the person has given us permission to use their name, the names are real.

- The stories are for informational purposes only. We're not saying we recommend you do what the person in the story did. Every situation's different, and we're sharing the stories and everything else to add tools to your toolbox. Only you can decide in any given situation what strategies you want to try.

- Throughout *Get Empowered*, you'll find definitions in the margins for terms you may not be familiar with. They're also collected in the Glossary starting on page 241.

- You can go to getempoweredbook.com and sign up to get bonus content, additional resources for working with the book, and more.

CLOSING

Congratulations again for reclaiming yourself and your life! We believe in you and your potential to bring more ease, more empowerment, and more healing to your life while you let go of shame, self-blame, and fear.

We've witnessed tens of thousands of students work through barriers to advocate for themselves and to transform themselves into strong people who can use their voices to be authentically themselves. They can say "no" to what they don't want and can ask for what they *do* want.

We're excited for you to do it too, and we're with you *every step* of the way!

YOU CAN'T POUR FROM AN EMPTY CUP.

Chapter 1

WHERE YOU'RE GOING

Envisioning the Life You Want

GROUNDING & CENTERING: The connection places. Pause for a minute. No matter what position you're in, feel where your body meets the world around it. It could be your feet or back on the floor, your butt in the chair, or anything else. Take a minute to feel each connection place. Now feel where your body touches your body, such as your hands on your thighs or your lips touching each other. Feel the texture, the temperature, the energy where they meet.

Before you start dismantling the barriers to self-advocacy, let's imagine the life you want. Having a vision of where you want to go can help you create the life you want and can be a touchstone as you do this work. We'll also help you build a path to get where you're going using patience, practice, self-compassion, and self-care.

PART 1

Where Do You Want to Go?

What would your life be like if the threat—or reality—of harassment, abuse, and assault weren't always with you?

Let's look at where you want to go. This process will help you go beyond avoiding pain to moving *toward* the life you want.

In 2018, feminist next door (@emrazz) asked her Twitter followers what they'd do if for twenty-four hours there were no men:

feminist next door
@emrazz

Women, imagine that for 24 hours, there were no men in the world.

No men are being harmed in the creation of this hypothetical. They will all return. They are safe and happy wherever they are during this hypothetical time period.

What would or could you do that day?

4:57 PM • DEC 24, 2018 • Twitter for iPhone

She posts this every year on Christmas Eve, and as of 2022, more than twenty thousand people have responded. The most common answer was that they'd go for a walk at night.

Jane Doe—she/her
@janedoe
Replying to @emrazz

Walk at night. Just walk. That's it.

5:35 PM • DEC 24, 2018 • Twitter for iPhone

A LIFE WITHOUT FEAR. Ask yourself: What would you do, how would you live your life, if you knew you'd be safe from harassment, abuse, and assault? Here are some examples to get you started, and you can fill in your own below:

- ☐ Go for a walk at night
- ☐ Set limits with my family
- ☐ Use my own identity in the digital space
- ☐ Wear what I want
- ☐ Live alone
- ☐ Post more online and share my opinions
- ☐ Go hiking or camping
- ☐ Go to a bar alone
- ☐ Stop constantly looking to see who's around me
- ☐ Go out dancing
- ☐ Leave my windows open at night
- ☐ Wear earbuds
- ☐ Leave my drink unattended
- ☐ Talk without watching my tone or making things more palatable for others
- ☐ Travel solo
- ☐ _____
- ☐ _____
- ☐ _____

Now take a more holistic look at how you'd like to live. We're looking beyond physical safety to emotional and mental safety—and belonging—as well. Pick a few items below and fill in the blanks, and then add your own.

- If I weren't afraid of being seen as rude, I'd _____

_____

- If I weren't afraid of being wrong, I'd _____

  _____

- If I could take up as much space as I wanted, I'd _____

  _____

- If I didn't worry about what other people think, I'd _____

  _____

- If I could say anything, I'd _____

  _____

- If my internal critic was silent, I'd _____

  _____

- If I didn't depend on someone else, I'd _____

  _____

- If other people would be supportive, I'd _____

  _____

- If I didn't feel my housing, grades, or job would be jeopardized, I'd _____

  _____

- If my family would be kind, respectful, and accepting, I'd _____

  _____

- If my partner would still love me, I'd _____

  _____

- If my friends would still care about me and include me, I'd _____

  _____

- If I could do anything, I'd _____

  _____

I LIKE MY LIFE. Think about your life now. How content are you with it? Write the things in your life that you're grateful for or that bring you joy (we've given some examples to get you started). Another way to think about it: If you were creating your life from scratch, what would you definitely want to include? (One way to imagine activities you'd like is to think of what you enjoyed when you were young—for example, doing hair on dolls or people, skateboarding, playing in the dirt, drawing, and so on.) Write or draw your answers below.

- Pets
- Friends
- Home
- Family
- Community
- School
- Work
- Faith

- Creative time: painting, drawing, sewing, quilting, baking, cooking, posting on social media (TikTok, etc.), woodworking...
- Games
- Movement/sports: biking, running, walking, basketball, rugby, canoeing, kayaking, rock climbing, dancing...

THE LIFE I WANT. What could you do without the limits that have been put on you by society, by media, by how you were raised? Imagine your life how you'd like it to be, without the limits that fear of harassment, abuse, and assault—or actual violence—put on all of us.

What would your life look like? Don't think about what's "realistic." Just imagine how you would shape your life if you could do anything.

Using the words and images from the exercises above, make a collage, vision board, drawing, painting, song, poem, or list that expresses your life without limits. When you're done (or done for now; you can keep adding to this over time), sit with your creation for a few minutes and observe your feelings.

Lauren's Story
A wobbly biker

I went on a weeklong bike trip with a group; one of the cyclists was Iris, who was in her seventies. Iris had had brain surgery, and because of it, was a bit unsteady on her feet and on her bike. Her whole family was against her going on the trip, and she carried with her letters from her adult children trying to talk her out of it. Iris rode more than fifty—sometimes wobbly—miles a day, and she had a blast! I don't know what she did to push through the limits others tried to put on her, but I was thrilled to witness her doing it.

PART 2

How to Get There

As you do the work of transforming your life, you'll find two things helpful: patience and practice.

Remember that we're up against a lifetime of conditioning and up against entire systems that benefit from us staying how we are. So celebrate the times you set a limit or ask for what you want—however small.

Strive to have compassion for and patience with yourself, where you've been, and the distance you still want to go. It's a process, and you're worth it. Changing years of conditioning isn't simple.

Learning any physical skill (rock climbing, martial arts, knitting, a new dance . . .) by repeating moves will at first feel awkward and unnatural. The goal of practicing is to make the moves familiar enough that they'll flow without thought.

Similarly, we can repeat ways of speaking, thinking, and behaving that may at first seem awkward but will become more natural with practice.

You might think of it as training for a race. You don't get up off the couch and start running. First you get up off the couch and walk around the block.

After doing that for a while, you might start walking for twenty to thirty minutes a day. When that starts to feel easy, you alternate jogging for five minutes and walking for five minutes. And so on . . . until you can do a 5K or a marathon—whatever's growth for you!

This work is training your assertiveness, boundary setting, and self-defense muscles, and the process is the same.

If you're in a relationship with someone who's abusing you, this may mean practicing in your head and heart and planning for the future. It's not necessary, or always helpful, to start with the most difficult situations we face.

Moving toward valuing ourselves is a first step. If you realize that you're being hard on yourself, take a deep breath and give yourself a hug. Treat yourself with the same compassion you would show someone you love, say some words of encouragement, take a break if you want, and keep going. (For more on negative self-talk and what to do with it, see Chapter 6.)

Focus on where you're going—and on the progress you've made!

Lauren's Story
Eyes up!

I took my first self-defense class when I was twenty-eight, and because of that class I realized that I looked down almost all the time. It felt really hard to look up and impossible to make eye contact. Instead of being hard on myself for it, I decided to treat it as useful information and work on it. I started by reminding myself to look up in low-stakes situations, like in the hallways at the office where I worked. I graduated to keeping my eyes at human level outside or when there were people around. Finally, I started working on keeping my eyes up when I was in a conversation. It took about a decade (!), but I learned to move through the world with my head up.

PART 3

Along the Way: Self-Care

**CARING FOR MYSELF IS NOT SELF-INDULGENCE,
IT IS SELF-PRESERVATION, AND THAT IS
AN ACT OF POLITICAL WARFARE.**

—Audre Lorde

This is hard stuff. As we do the challenging work of healing from the damage the patriarchy has done to us and claiming our power, it's important to take care of ourselves.

Self-care is anything you do to take care of your mental, emotional, physical, and spiritual well-being. Self-care looks different for every person, and you probably already know some things that work for you.

Still, self-care can be easier said than done. Society and capitalism glorify productivity and achievement. It tells all of us, especially women, that taking time for ourselves or putting ourselves first is selfish. We're supposed to be on, and giving, all the time. We're told we must earn our time off, and even then, that rest is an indulgence.

That can stand in the way of attending to our well-being. So can lack of time or money. Not everyone has money for a manicure or even time for a bath (and not everyone has a bathtub), for example. Self- and community care have been made consumerist, have been commodified. Self-care has become something you *buy,* like massages, vacations, and bath bombs.

Even things that don't cost money, like doing yoga at home or spending time in nature, are not equally available to people of all classes, races, and abilities. Self-care can also seem like a burden: one more thing on the to-do list. And if we do it and we don't feel better, we're told there's something wrong with us.

What's more, self-care can reinforce the notion that our well-being is entirely up to us—

Patriarchy is a social system in which cisgender men hold primary power and predominate in roles of political leadership, moral authority, social privilege, and control of property. In patriarchal societies, men largely hold the power and women are largely excluded from it.

that it doesn't have to do with the realities of race, gender, class, and more that profoundly affect our lives.

Even if finances or time commitments limit your access to self-care, it's an important part of surviving in an often-hostile world. We can't wait until White supremacy and patriarchy are dismantled to be able to rest. And because we're asking you to look at some difficult issues and experiences, we encourage you to consciously pay attention to your well-being while working with this book. Within whatever constraints you have, we suggest you intentionally seek to integrate some ease, joy, and comfort into your life while doing this work. Find ways to care for yourself, to soothe yourself, to honor yourself, to take time for yourself as much as you can.

Especially for survivors, whose nervous systems are often stuck in fight, flight, or freeze mode, anything we can do to relax is helpful. (To learn more about fight, flight, and freeze, see Chapter 8.) As part of healing, taking back our power, and sustaining ourselves to do this work, we encourage you to have a self-care plan.

HOW WILL I CARE FOR MYSELF? As you work with this book, make self-care, rest, well-being, and joy your priorities. What self-care do you already do? What self-care might you add?

Here are some types of self-care; put a check mark next to the ones you already do and a star next to the ones you'd like to add to your routine or do more of. Then write in other self-care ideas that work for you.

- ☐ Be in nature
- ☐ Create a vision board
- ☐ Do the dishes
- ☐ Play cards or host a game night
- ☐ Draw, paint, do a jigsaw puzzle, or knit
- ☐ Exercise, walk, do yoga, dance, stretch, or do other movement
- ☐ Garden or care for houseplants
- ☐ Go to bed early, sleep late, take a nap

☐ Get my prescriptions filled

☐ Sing with friends

☐ Hug or snuggle with someone I love (this includes a pet!)

☐ Journal or make a gratitude list

☐ Work with a therapist

☐ Delete unnecessary items from my to-do list

☐ Laugh; watch a funny movie or some stand-up

☐ Listen to music or nature sounds

☐ Meditate, notice my breathing, or pray

☐ Put my phone away

☐ Read or listen to books, poems, or podcasts

☐ Say "no" to something I don't want to do

☐ Set and keep boundaries about when I answer calls, emails, texts, etc.
from my job

☐ Spend time with someone I care about

☐ Stop reading the comments

☐ Take time off, whether an evening, a day, a weekend, or longer

☐ Turn off social media

☐ Watch the clouds, the stars, or a sunrise or sunset

☐ _____

☐ _____

☐ _____

☐ _____

☐ _____

☐ _____

☐ _____

TL;DR

- TL;DR, or to make a long story short, we invite you to chart a course to a bigger, more confident, safer life.

- We suggest you embrace practicing and having patience along the way.

- We also encourage you to have a self-care plan as you work with *Get Empowered*, and we offer some guidance for creating one.

THE HEART OF THE MATTER. *What's your main takeaway from this chapter? Write it down, text it to a friend, draw it. However you choose to summarize or remember it, thinking about it now will help you as you make change for yourself.*

SELF-CARE BREAK. *Take a deep breath. What self-care will you do now that you've finished this chapter? It can be a small thing (like a few seconds of stretching) or something bigger (like a day off). For more ideas, check in with the plan you made on page xix or the ideas we list on page 10.*

SAY "YES" TO YOURSELF. *Self-care—and this whole book—is about saying "yes" to yourself. It's a way of respecting yourself, of recognizing that you're human. You deserve all of it.*

Chapter 2

MORE THAN RAPE

Understanding the Problem

GROUNDING & CENTERING: Energy center. Rub your hands together, creating some energy and heat. Then pat your body to transfer the energy to any spots that are holding stress, like your lower back or feet. Rub your hands together again, then rest your palms lightly over your eyes. Finally, shake out your hands, releasing the energy.

Before we start making change, we first need to understand what we're up against. What is gender-based violence, and why does it exist? What role does it play in society? We'll answer those questions because they provide crucial context for understanding our own feelings, choices, behaviors, and more.

YOU HAVE A RIGHT TO BE SAFE.

PART 1

What Is Gender-Based Violence?

Most people think of gender-based violence as rape, sexual assault, and physical abuse in relationships. That's true, but it's also much more.

Problematic behaviors fall on a spectrum, and they're all part of gender-based violence. This spectrum doesn't include *everything,* but it includes some of the most common ways gender-based violence shows up.

Some behaviors on the spectrum—hugging, for example—might be problematic only when there's no consent or when the act is manipulative rather than honest.

No behavior has a "right" spot on the spectrum. You may feel differently about each one than other people do, and how you feel about it can vary minute to minute. Where a behavior falls on the spectrum for you depends on many factors, like the context it's happening in, your relationship with the person doing it, and what you've already been through. Trust your own experience to determine where these behaviors live for you.

Before looking at the spectrum, please take a few seconds to breathe and feel your feet if you can.

Consent is when everyone involved wants something and agrees that it's okay. For example, if you say, "Is it okay if I hug you?" and the other person says, "Sure!" then you've both consented to a hug, but that doesn't mean a kiss is okay. Either of you can also change your mind mid-hug or make a different decision about hugs in the future. Consent isn't only about physical or sexual contact; it applies to almost everything that involves more than one person, like what time they can text you, whether you can tag them in a photo, whether you want them to take off their shoes in your home, whether you're okay with them sharing information about you, and more.

Not listening to "NO" could fall anywhere on the spectrum. In many ways, it's the BIGGEST RED FLAG. If you set a limit and the other person won't or can't accept it, that tells you A LOT about their respect for you and their intentions.

Hitting me, pushing me, choking me, or beating me up

Forcing me to have sex with other people

Raping or sexually assaulting me

Threatening to out me
(my sex assigned at birth, sexual orientation, immigration status, etc.)

Threatening to take the kids

Threatening to hurt my family or friends

COULD KILL YOU

Removing or puncturing a condom during sex (stealthing)

Threatening to harm themselves if I won't do what they want

Refusing to use protection when we're having sex

Trying to get me drunk or high to get me to have sex

Controlling all our money

Discouraging or stopping me from seeing my friends or family

Getting mad if they think I look at other people

Getting angry if things aren't "just right"

Not listening to "no"

Always wanting to know where I am, what I'm doing, or who I'm with

Sexualizing certain races or ethnic groups (for example, saying Latinas are "spicy" or Asian women are "submissive")

Mistreating my pet

Throwing or destroying my things

Showing up when I don't want them to (stalking)

Taking photos under my skirt or dress without permission (upskirting)

Touching me or grabbing me when I don't want them to

DANGEROUS

Yelling at me

Bullying me online or in person

Asking about trans people's genitals

Grinding up against me without asking or after I've said "no"

Sexting me even though I asked them not **to**

Recording me without my consent

Calling me names or slurs

Sharing naked photos of me without permission

Making me feel afraid, stupid, or bad about myself

Showing their genitals in public

Insulting me, criticizing me, or putting me down

Spreading sexual rumors about me or other people

Sending unsolicited naked photos

Putting me down in front of our friends

Looking in windows

Invading my personal space or standing too close

Slut-shaming me or others

Staring or leering

Touching me to move me out of the way

Telling "jokes" about girls/women, LGBTQIA+ people, or fat people

ANNOYING

Harassing me on the street or public **transit**

Interrupting me or talking over me

Expecting me to move out of their way in public spaces

It might be hard to see how a harassing text message has anything to do with rape, but if we think more deeply, we'll see that all these behaviors are related, and they have a lot in common. Let's take a look.

THEY'RE ALL UNWANTED

Some of these behaviors would be absolutely fine if both people were into it—if consent were asked for and enthusiastically given. Think, for example, of sexts. It's the fact that they're unwanted that makes them a problem.

THEY ALL INVADE OUR SPACE

These behaviors all invade our space, whether physically, emotionally, or spiritually. When someone touches us without our permission, our personal space has been violated. When someone mentally undresses us or verbally harasses us, they may be intending to make us lower our eyes, to shrink, and to remind us that we don't really have the right to our own bodies or to be in the workplace or in public places, including online.

Even without touching, things like manspreading, unwanted comments about our bodies, or being leered at make many of us give up our space. We change our route, move to another seat on public transportation, avoid jobs with late hours, or are afraid to live alone. Our worlds get smaller, and we get used to taking up little space or giving up the space we have taken.

THEY'RE ALL BASED ON GENDER IDENTITY OR SEXUAL ORIENTATION

Although everything on this spectrum is based on gender identity or sexual orientation, these behaviors will take different forms for those of us with other marginalized identities. For example, harassment of Black women is usually both racist and sexist (a combination known as *misogynoir*). Lesbians and trans men are the most likely to be targeted for so-called corrective rape, which attackers believe is a punishment for their identities or somehow will make them straight and cisgender.

The more marginalized identities a person or group has, the more likely they are to be targeted. So, for example, Indigenous women, bisexual women, trans women of color (especially Black and Latina trans women), and people with disabilities (including intellectual disabilities) experience the most frequent and severe gender-based violence in the U.S. We could also create spectrums for violence based on other types of oppression, like ableism, racism, religious persecution, and more.

Cisgender describes anyone who identifies with the sex they were assigned at birth; someone who isn't transgender. Also called *cis*.

Ableism is prejudice and discrimination against people with disabilities; valuing nondisabled people more.

Racism is individual and systemic bias or discrimination against Black, Indigenous, Latine, Asian, and other people of color based on the belief that White identity is the norm and that BIPOC are lesser, problematic, or abnormal.

THEY ALL CAN ESCALATE

Everything along the spectrum can escalate. Even actions most people might think of as just annoying (like staring) can lead to things that are dangerous or life-threatening. For example, a coworker or boss asking personal questions can lead to verbal harassment. That can lead to unwanted touching, which might lead to sexual assault. A partner who doesn't want you to see friends or family can turn into a stalker.

Behaviors can escalate over minutes, days, or years—and escalation doesn't always go in a straight line.

The truth is, the behaviors lower on the spectrum happen often—sometimes every day or more than once a day (like street harassment). It's often tempting to let them slide because they can seem like no big deal. But they do interfere with our lives, and if we take action, we may have a chance of stopping them from getting worse.

THEY ALL EXPRESS, GAIN, OR MAINTAIN POWER AND CONTROL

These behaviors express dominance over or disrespect for another person's bodily integrity and autonomy, feelings, or needs. When done by men, they reinforce men's power, whether that be their "right" to touch, manipulate, invade space, intimidate, harass, hit, or rape. Our society encourages toxic masculinity by encouraging men to gain self-worth from power over others.

Assault, sexual and otherwise, also bolsters power and control based on race, ethnicity, religion, class, age, size, sexual orientation, gender, immigration status, mental and physical disabilities, and more.

Invading someone's space, especially with touching, is an expression of power. Who has the right to touch whom shows who has the power. Think about the workplace: Many bosses would go up to a worker and throw their arm around that worker's shoulder. But it's very unusual for the opposite to happen. Similarly, a White person is more likely to touch a Black or Brown person than the reverse.

When we're touched without consent, that reinforces who has the power in the situation (even though both people may be unconscious of the touching or how it relates to power). That may bolster a sense of powerlessness in those who are targeted and make it difficult for us to believe in our ability to protect ourselves.

Behaviors on the higher end of the spectrum are more obvious statements of the power of men over women and children; the power of straight, cis people over LGBTQIA+ people; the power of White people over Black, Indigenous, and people of color (BIPOC); and so on.

Physical, emotional, sexual, and financial abuse, harassment, stalking, rape, and trafficking all remind us of the power other groups of people have over us (and that we have over others)—and these behaviors reinforce that power imbalance.

BIPOC stands for Black, Indigenous, and people of color. Unlike the terms *people of color* or *POC*, it highlights the fact that the U.S. was founded on the enslavement of Black people and the genocide of Indigenous peoples. The term encompasses all marginalized racial and ethnic groups, including Black, Indigenous, Latine, and Asian/Pacific Islander people; people can have more than one of these identities.

This is especially true when the aggressor has status in the community or power to retaliate if we tell anyone else about what's happening, and when the person targeted has identities or social roles that give them less power.

THEY ALL LEAVE US FEELING BAD

We can feel all kinds of ways after being the target of one or more of these behaviors—upset, afraid, angry, shocked, ashamed, humiliated, helpless, powerless, enraged, and confused are common feelings.

And any boundary violation can remind us of past experiences.

THEY ALL DESENSITIZE US TO FURTHER VIOLATION

Because these behaviors are so common and often don't escalate, they become normal, everyday realities. We become used to looks, gestures, touches, or words that could be clues that something more serious may be about to happen.

We also become used to the behaviors on the spectrum because society denies that many of them are problems, even seeing some as "jokes." Media portrayals of gender-based violence—as well as more subtle negative stereotypes about women, people of color, LGBTQIA+ people, people with disabilities, fat people, and others—can make some of these behaviors seem normal to the point we don't even notice them. Acceptance of the lesser forms of disrespect allows more dangerous behavior.

For example, when boys grab girls at school (over and over again), many girls are taught to treat it as a joke, even though they usually don't really feel it's funny. And some people see extreme jealousy as a sign of love instead of as the controlling behavior it is; many rom-coms encourage this belief.

This doesn't mean the world can be divided up into targets and aggressors. Most of us have crossed someone's boundaries or treated someone disrespectfully. Most of us have done that to ourselves (through self-hatred, self-harm, or lack of self-care).

Mature, healthy people take action—to be accountable, apologize and/or forgive, and change our behavior. Those who mistreat others, on the other hand, justify their actions and feel entitled to harass, abuse, and attack, and they blame everyone but themselves. Their apologies are fleeting and don't lead to real change.

BY THE NUMBERS

Probably every single one of us was warned about "stranger danger" when we were little. And for our whole lives, popular culture and news media have distorted our perceptions of danger, leading us to feel fear around parking lots, alleys, and bushes (think *Law & Order: SVU*, all the *CSIs*, true-crime podcasts and docuseries, and the evening news).

Though attacks by people we don't know in public places do happen, the fact is that most gender-based violence is committed by someone we know.

Obviously, if it's partner abuse, 100% of those being abused know their abusers.

And for women, almost 90% of all rapes are by someone the woman knows. Louder for those in the back: NINE OUT OF TEN FEMALE RAPE SURVIVORS KNOW THEIR ATTACKERS.

Why does this matter?

SO YOU CAN PAY ATTENTION TO WHERE THE REAL DANGERS OF GENDER-BASED VIOLENCE ARE. Danger lies (in this order) with current or former partners, with acquaintances (like coworkers, friends and friends of friends, neighbors, etc.), and with other family members and strangers. By paying attention to how these people treat us and how we feel when we're around them, we can notice (and notice sooner) signs that something's not right or that we're uncomfortable.

SO YOU CAN FEEL LESS FEAR. Once you know where the risks *really lie* and how to identify them, you can be more relaxed in other parts of your life. The problem mostly isn't in parking lots, dark alleys, or bushes. Here's what you might want to know about gender-based violence.

Two-thirds of sexual violence happens in or near the victim's home or the home of a friend or relative.

Nine out of ten attackers don't have a weapon.

More than half of the time (55%) the aggressor is the same race as the person they're targeting (see "Especially If You're White: Spidey Sense and Racism" on page 93 for more on this).

55% same race | 45% other race

The reality is different for Indigenous women and men, whose attackers are much more likely to be White men than someone Indigenous, and much more likely to be a stranger.

Unfortunately, no data on aggressor-target relationships is available for non-binary people; the number of non-binary people is relatively small, and most researchers aren't yet asking inclusive questions.

PART 2

Framework: Why Is This Even Happening?

When our boundaries have been crossed or when we've been violated, many of us will think it's happening because of something we did wrong or a personal failing. This isn't true!

Violence, whether microaggressions (like staring, pressing on a woman's back to move her out of the way, or touching a Black woman's hair without permission) or more intense (like emotional abuse or a physical attack), is an expression of the power imbalances in society. It's also a way to maintain those power imbalances. Violence benefits the group that has power over another group.

> *Gender-based violence isn't just a personal problem.*
> *It's part of a system of oppression.*

And oppression—the power imbalances—isn't just a few (or a bunch of) people with biased beliefs. It's prejudice plus power.

Sexism, racism, and other systems of oppression are a result of the larger systems of patriarchy and White supremacy. These systems give those groups with more power (for example, men, straight people, and White people) advantages and rights that the people in oppressed groups don't have in the political, social, economic, and other spheres. (And, of course, many people belong to more than one oppressed group).

Patriarchy, White supremacy, xenophobia, ableism, and other interconnected systems of oppression

Xenophobia is fear, hatred, or mistreatment of people from other countries or cultures.

make those in the oppressed group more likely to be targeted for harassment, abuse, assault, and other kinds of violence.

This is true for all systems of oppression: oppressed people depend on the approval and goodwill of those in power for our livelihoods, even our lives. So anything we do to rock the boat may endanger us. For example, we often can't risk challenging a boss, landlord, or caseworker; if we did, we might lose income, housing, benefits, or other things we need to survive. If we speak openly about sexual abuse in our family, we may be thrown out—depriving us of housing, health care, and more.

Society reinforces those power imbalances by denying or minimizing our experiences, silencing us, and making us lose trust in ourselves. We're blamed for our own suffering, which uses up a tremendous amount of our energy.

Media and the culture in general reinforce these beliefs. Other ways rape culture shows up include:

- Cultural representations, such as those depicting Black women as hypersexual and Asian women as exotic or submissive, using women's bodies to sell products, or "jokes" about sluts or virgins in the media

- Institutions (like many religions and the criminal legal system) that, for example, encourage staying in a relationship with an abuser, allow a survivor's sexual history to be part of a rape prosecution, or hide the acts of abuse within their own organizations and give no consequences to those doing harm

- Beliefs that minimize the effects of violence, like "That was a long time ago—aren't you over it?" or "It's no big deal—just some unwanted sex," or "Women regret sex and call it rape"

- Framing the problem as an individual one; for example, believing that only deviants or pathological people commit violence

- Victim-blaming, such as politicians or judges saying, "You can't thread a moving needle," or "It takes two to tango," meaning that the victim-survivor must have "wanted it"

- Gender socialization and rigid gender roles, such as girls being taught not to believe in their power or that assertiveness is a negative quality, or boys being taught not to show sadness or vulnerability and that strength is the most important quality.

Victim-blaming, shame, and silence about what's happening allow the violence to keep happening. If the focus is on the victim's behavior, the victim is the one whose behavior is being controlled.

As a result of all this, violence reinforces powerlessness and keeps women, LGBTQIA+ people, other gender-diverse people, and other oppressed groups in "their place."

Gender socialization is the process of teaching people how to behave according to gender roles. For example, gender stereotypes encouraging girls to be passive (girls are praised for being "good" and "nice") and boys to be aggressive (infant boys are played with more roughly than infant girls) or saying that girls are good at people skills and boys are good at sports and math. Parents, schools, and the media are the most common ways we learn what roles we're supposed to fill.

Physical assault or abuse isn't necessary to achieve these effects. Fear of violence is an important control mechanism that's effective even without physical violence. Self-blame allows violence to continue because it draws focus from the true reasons for gender-based violence.

Especially If You're White
Racism and rape

Throughout European history, women were treated as property. Husband and wife were seen as one, and that *one* was the husband. During slavery in the United States, the state considered Black women to be the legal property of White men, and those White men sexually and reproductively exploited them. We still live in a society descended from this history, and Black men and women today suffer disproportionately from it.

Since White people colonized what became the United States and started participating in the transatlantic slave trade and enslaving Black people, White men have targeted Black men for supposed threats to the "virtue" of the White women who "belonged" to them. White men created and perpetuated a myth of

Black men as animalistic, sexual monsters. Black men were demonized for any attention—real or imagined—they gave White women, even for looking in the direction of a White woman, or sometimes for doing *literally* nothing at all. Often, White women were (and are) complicit in this demonization. The punishment for these supposed crimes was often death, whether by the government or by vigilantes.

The myth of the "dangerous Black man" has been used to harm, lock up, and kill Black men throughout this country's history—even though most violence is *intra*racial (meaning the aggressor and the target are of the same race).

Though slavery has formally ended in the U.S. (except in the prison system), these dynamics continue. White people often see Black and Brown men as hypersexual and a threat to women—especially White women. They don't see White men as the same kind of threat. Media forms and reinforces that view daily. One result is that White women often harm Black and Brown men in response to behaviors they wouldn't find threatening coming from a White man (like walking behind them on the sidewalk); that harm can look like, for example, crossing the street to avoid someone, clutching a purse, or calling the police.

When slavery was legal, it wasn't a crime to rape an enslaved person. Black women, like Black men, were seen as hypersexual and animalistic. Because of this myth, and the legalized "ownership" of Black bodies, the White legal system considered Black women "unrapable." Enslavers—and the law—held that you can't rape someone who doesn't have autonomy, or someone who's seen as always sexually available and a "temptress." The babies that resulted from these rapes were considered White men's property.

To this day, Black girls are seen as more adult, more sexual, than White girls, and thus more sexually available and more to blame for what happens to them. Black women's victimization often is minimized and ignored, erasing their experiences and blocking them from getting justice in any form.

Society doesn't value the bodies of women of color as much as it does those of White women, so violations against them aren't treated as seriously. Black and Brown women are also much more likely to be locked up for defending themselves than White women are for the same actions.

Over many years, society and racism have taught White women to be afraid of Black and Brown men. When White women change our behavior because of that fear, we're perpetuating racism. We're also not making ourselves any safer. White women also perpetuate racism when we fail to push back against stereotypes about Black women. (See "Especially If You're White: Spidey Sense and Racism" in Chapter 5 for more on this.)

PART 3

Speak Out: Some of What We've Been Through

Take a look at the stories below. They come from our own experiences and those of our friends, family members, and students. We'll work with these stories throughout the book. After reading them, please write an experience of your own.

Take a minute to get grounded and do some self-care before reading these stories, because they describe painful experiences. Maybe you want to call a friend before you start, make some tea, grab a comfy blanket, do some stretches, or set a timer to remind yourself to take a break.

If reading them starts to feel like too much, pause or skip ahead to the next part of the book.

Kailin was staying with her aunt and uncle while she checked out colleges in their city. One night, as they all were going upstairs to bed, Kailin's uncle put his hand on her butt, joking that he was "helping" her up the stairs. She screamed in surprise and thought he got the message that she wasn't okay with it. But in the middle of the night, she woke up and he was lying in bed with her. She froze out of fear and said nothing. In the morning, she didn't know what to do because she didn't have anywhere else to go, and she wasn't sure if she should say anything to her aunt.

Tiffani went to her family doctor for a checkup when she was sixteen. She'd known him most of her life because their families belonged to the same immigrant community. At one point he mentioned how grown up and "womanly" she was becoming. At first his compliments felt good, even though she was a bit uncomfortable. When he asked more about her relationship with her boyfriend, Tiffani said nothing beyond mumbling politely. The doctor finished the checkup and ended with a tight hug, saying something about how amazing chemistry between two people can be. When Tiffani told her parents she didn't want to see him anymore and why, they said they didn't want to switch doctors because they thought it was important to see someone who spoke their primary language. They said they were glad they had a doctor who knew them so well, they were sure he didn't "mean anything" by his comments, and that she shouldn't make a big deal out of it.

Yasmeen was home alone when a neighbor came to the door and asked for her help. He said that his wife had been in an accident and he was on the way to the hospital. He needed to pick up his daughter at a friend's apartment and wanted Yasmeen to go along so she could take care of the daughter at the hospital. He said he knew his daughter saw Yasmeen as an aunt or older sister, so he'd thought of her. Yasmeen thought it was a little strange, but as she was reconsidering, he told her he so appreciated having someone he could count on— "it's so rare these days." Besides, he seemed truly upset and she *was* concerned for the girl. She agreed to help for just a while. They went to the friend's house to get his daughter, but no one was there. He opened it with a key and invited her to wait with him until his daughter came back from the park. Once inside, he robbed and raped her. She told her school counselor, but since her neighbor was known in the neighborhood as a "good guy," the counselor told her she must be exaggerating. She didn't tell anyone else.

Ashlie was raising two children alone after her husband left. She wasn't feeling very good about herself, so when Evan, a prominent member of her church, started showing interest in her, she was thrilled. He seemed to love her children, treated her like a queen, and was everything she'd ever dreamed of. He pushed quickly to get married. Evan was extremely jealous of any man she talked to and questioned her about where she was going and where she'd been; Ashlie saw these as signs of his love. Shortly after the marriage, Evan started using verbal put-downs—and eventually physical violence. But he always apologized and seemed sincerely sorry. When he wasn't being abusive, he was wonderful. And Ashlie wanted her children to have a father in their lives. A few years later, Evan started to abuse the children, and Ashlie decided she needed help. She didn't know where to turn, since everyone in her church loved him and people told her that it was her responsibility to hold the family together. She certainly didn't want to break up the family like her first husband had, so she resolved to try harder.

LaKeisha, who was in the last year of middle school, was at a high school party. Some older guys were there and she really wanted them to like her. She drank beer because she wanted to fit in, and she liked how it felt when she drank. She couldn't believe it when Caleb, who was one of the popular kids, paid attention to her. She was especially excited because both adults and other kids teased her about her weight, and she was flattered that Caleb found her attractive. Throughout the night he kept bringing her more beer and dancing with her. When she started to feel sick, he suggested that she lie down upstairs. She passed out and woke up with his penis inside her. The rape was her first sexual experience, and she was devastated. She believed she had "asked for it" by drinking and flirting with an older guy. She didn't tell anyone because her parents would be angry at her for drinking, and her friends all thought Caleb was the greatest and would never believe her. She had heard them putting down other girls who had "cried rape" and ruined a guy's reputation; they also said things like "Guys would never go for fat girls, they're so desperate they make things up."

Yessica's disabilities meant she needed help with things like getting dressed and making meals. It was really difficult finding a personal assistant she liked, and when a friend's cousin volunteered to help after school, she was grateful. In the beginning, Trinity seemed fine. Trinity was gentle with Yessica and seemed concerned about her feelings. Then one day when Trinity was helping move her, Trinity's hand stayed near Yessica's breast too long. Yessica didn't say anything since she wasn't sure what was happening. Over the weeks, Trinity crossed more lines physically, and Yessica often felt humiliated and slightly afraid. She didn't speak up though, because she was afraid Trinity would complain about her and leave before she could find another aide.

Chris met Raena on an app. After only a couple of weeks, Raena started asking Chris for his passwords, saying it was "a sign of trust." Since Chris was really into Raena and felt like they might have a future together, he felt okay about sharing his social passwords. But when Raena asked for money-related passwords (like for his bank), Chris was hesitant. Not long after that, Raena started asking Chris for money directly: first for her rent, next for a vet bill, then to go visit her sick brother . . . there was always a desperate reason she needed money. Chris was sympathetic, but Raena's needs got to be too much, especially since they'd only known each other a little while. Chris broke up with Raena, but she wouldn't let go. She texted dozens of times a day and started showing up at Chris's work, getting him in trouble with his boss. Chris was afraid to set a limit because every time he'd done it before, Raena had only ramped up her demands.

Alexis's partner, Elena, was moody, and Alexis walked on eggshells sometimes to keep Elena happy. When they argued, Elena would fly into a rage; she accused Alexis of being unsupportive and disloyal. The controlling behavior got worse to the point that Elena grabbed Alexis and left bruises on them. Afterward, Elena apologized and begged Alexis not to leave. Other times, Elena would cry and tell Alexis about her awful childhood. Alexis was confused and scared but still had good times with Elena and did care about her. Alexis's job paid for some counseling, and Alexis suggested the two of them go. Elena refused, saying Alexis had to be "less sensitive." Besides, Elena didn't want to take their couple problems to someone who might not understand queer relationships. Finally, Alexis said they were going to end the relationship, and Elena threatened to kill herself. Elena said Alexis was the only one who understood her, and she couldn't live without them.

Laila worked in a restaurant, and her manager had been crossing her boundaries by saying sexist and racist things for a while, including that he "liked the taste of chocolate." Laila didn't say anything about it because she was trying to get a promotion, and the manager seemed to be ready to give her one. One day the manager said that he and another manager wanted to talk with Laila about the promotion, and they invited her to dinner. When she got in the car with him, he took her hand and put it on his thigh. That's when she saw he had his penis out. She was shocked and didn't know what to do. Later, she complained to another manager about being harassed, but instead of doing anything about it, they started cutting her shifts.

MY STORY. Briefly describe an experience of your own that you'd like to work with (if you like, you can expand in a journal).

Don't choose the most harmful thing that's ever happened to you—it needn't even be something you'd call assault. For example, it could be a situation where harassment left you with a bad feeling about yourself or the other person, or maybe a time you were pressured, but not forced, to go further than you wanted to sexually. Because we won't be focusing on physical self-defense skills, please don't choose an experience that *began* with a physical assault.

_____

_____

_____

_____

_____

As you complete exercises throughout the book, feel free to change the situation you're working with. You may also work on a less-harmful experience while keeping a more serious one in mind. How you do this work is entirely up to you.

TL;DR

- Gender-based violence is more than sexual assault and abuse in relationships. It's many behaviors on a spectrum from less violent (like staring) to full-on attack, from individual acts to those of hate groups. Understanding this is important because the so-called small things build up—affecting our lives and well-being—and because they can be precursors to more dangerous behaviors.

- Gender-based violence, like other forms of violence that enforce oppression, is a societal, not just personal, problem. It's a manifestation of gender oppression and a way of maintaining unequal power systems.

- Most gender-based violence is committed by someone we know. Related and also important: the person being targeted is usually the same race as the aggressor.

- Okay, one more thing: We want to remind you that no matter what you do or don't do, it's never your fault if someone harasses, abuses, or attacks you. No exceptions.

THE HEART OF THE MATTER. *What's the best or most important thing you're taking away from this chapter? It could be an idea, a realization, an understanding . . . anything new. Remember, you don't have to write it here. You can draw, doodle, tell a friend, record it on your phone, use a journal, or do whatever works for you.*

SELF-CARE BREAK. *Take a deep breath. What self-care will you do now that you've finished this chapter? It can be a small thing (like a few seconds of stretching) or something bigger (like a day off). For more ideas, check in with the plan you made on page xix or the ideas we list on page 10.*

WE BELIEVE IN YOU! *We know this can be a lot to take in. Please applaud (and maybe hug!) yourself for deciding to take the first step. It's a courageous and self-loving act.*

HARASSMENT, ABUSE, AND ASSAULT ARE NEVER YOUR FAULT. THE RESPONSIBILITY FOR THEM LIES 100% WITH THE PERSON WHO DOES THEM.

Chapter 3

HOW GENDER-BASED VIOLENCE HAPPENS

GROUNDING & CENTERING: Pay attention to your breath. You might feel the sensation of air going in and out of your nose, or your chest and belly expanding and contracting. You might pause slightly at the top of the in breath or the bottom of the out breath. Take three deep breaths while you consciously track their path through your body.

By understanding how abuse and assault commonly happen, we're more likely to spot the signs early and to have a chance of interrupting them. Here we'll break down the stages of abuse and assault. We'll also examine the ploys and parting shots aggressors often use and other red flags that can alert us to danger.

PART 1

The Stages of Assault

Most assaults, including abuse by partners, don't involve someone using physical violence suddenly or right away. Usually several things happen before the physical violence starts. The stages tend to go like this: select, approach and test, isolate, assault, and follow-up. They can happen over minutes, years, or anything in between.

STAGE 1: SELECT

First, the aggressor looks for someone they think won't resist or push back, who won't question their behavior, who'll be passive and compliant. This is called the selection stage.

When choosing someone to target, aggressors are looking for someone who's vulnerable. Vulnerability can take many forms, and what these forms have in common is that the people seen as vulnerable have less power, are less valued by society, and are less likely to be believed. Here are some of the factors seen as vulnerable; many of them overlap.

IDENTITY

This is where oppression plays the biggest role. Those who are systematically marginalized or excluded in one or several ways are often targeted because their status as a member of an oppressed group affords them less power.

So, for example, trans women of color (especially Black and Latina trans women), bisexual women, disabled people, and Indigenous women experience the most frequent and severe gender-based violence in the U.S. Children and young people are also abused at higher rates than those age twenty-five and older.

ROLE

People who have less power because of their roles are also more likely to be targeted, such as employees (versus bosses), congregation members (versus clergy), students (versus teachers or coaches), sex workers (versus law enforcement and clients), patients (versus doctors), immigrants (versus immigration officials), and those charged with a crime (versus police, lawyers, and judges). Those in systems or institutions (such as prison, the military, or a psychiatric hospital) are also more likely to be targeted.

PROXIMITY AND ACCESS

Most aggressors target someone who they're close to—physically or otherwise. Common targets include relatives, someone in a friend group, or a coworker. People can also be accessible to an aggressor because of where they live or work, as hotel housekeepers, domestic workers, and real estate agents are.

CAPACITY

Those who are less able to explain what happened to them are also more likely to be targeted. That can include children, people who don't speak fluent English, people with some types of mental illness or intellectual disabilities, and people who were drunk or high when the assault happened.

Among others seen as vulnerable are those who are lonely or have low self-esteem, single parents, and people living in poverty (including unhoused people).

STAGE 2: APPROACH AND TEST

During this stage, the aggressor may use tricks or ploys to get close, whether that means on the street, at school or work, or in a relationship. In some cases they're already close, physically or emotionally; for example, in a workplace, friend group, or family.

Sometimes when someone intends to do harm, they first build trust and break down boundaries to get closer to the person they want to target. During this time, they're friendly, helpful, and trustworthy, and they work to build a connection. They get the person they're targeting used to boundary violations, unwanted sexual conversation or images, and other problematic behaviors. (We'll talk more about red flags later in this chapter.) When this process is used to talk about what an adult does to a child, it's called *grooming*, and aggressors often use similar strategies with adults.

After selecting a person to target and approaching them, aggressors usually test whether the person they're targeting will go along—that is, be a "good victim"—or whether they'll push back and set boundaries. Testing usually looks like any kind of less violent boundary crossing; often it's one of the behaviors lower on the spectrum of gender-based violence (see Chapter 2). Here are some examples:

- Asking personal questions. "Do you live alone?" "If you don't mind my asking, what's your bra size?" "Do you have a boyfriend?" "Do your parents know you're queer?"

- Invading your physical space. Standing too close or initiating unwanted touching (such as touching your hair, your forearm, or your back, or grinding on you on the dance floor without consent).

- Saying something inappropriate (and often something sexual), like "They say redheads are hot in bed," "Have you ever tried anal?" "So I heard you go both ways," "Does your partner trust you?" Sometimes street harassment is a test to see what more the harasser can get away with.

- Telling an offensive, oppressive "joke."

- Trying to scare you. "You know I'm twice your size, right?"

After doing one of these problematic things, the aggressor watches how the potential victim reacts. Do they look uncomfortable? Do they speak up? Do they move or leave? Do they ignore the boundary crossing? That gives the aggressor information about whether a potential victim will be easily intimidated or coerced, or if they're likely to resist.

Many of the tests are subtle, allowing an aggressor, if confronted, to claim they weren't doing anything.

STEP 3: ISOLATE

Most sexual assault (as well as abuse and some harassment) doesn't happen out in the open. Aggressors isolate their targets before carrying out an assault. This can happen before, along with, or after the approach and testing.

STEP 4: ASSAULT

This is when the physical attack happens, and it looks like pretty much anything on the higher half of the spectrum in Chapter 2.

When people think of sexual assault, they usually think of the attacker using physical force. But it's important to realize that attackers mostly use threats, coercion, manipulation, and intimidation—along with substances, usually alcohol—to get those they've targeted to submit.

They also exploit any power differences to get what they want, such as between adult and child, employer and employee, teacher and student, or White person and person of color.

STEP 5: FOLLOW-UP

After the attack, an aggressor will often follow up with the victim-survivor to minimize the chances that they'll be held accountable for what they did. For example, they might say things like:

- "Nobody would believe you if you said anything." (People in positions of authority and elders especially use this.)

- "Nobody would believe anyone would want to have sex with someone who's [insert insult or slur here]. Don't flatter yourself."

- "You think I'd even be interested in you? I can't believe you're accusing me of this."

- "What's the matter? You don't like men?"

> **Gaslighting** is manipulating someone psychologically to try to get them to question their own reality, memory, sanity, experience, or perceptions. Most often seen in relationships where one person is being abusive, it also can be used in other situations where power is being abused, for example, after a rape.

Attackers also gaslight victim-survivors to keep them from speaking up. For example, an attacker might text and say, "That was so much fun! When do you want to get together again?" to make a victim-survivor doubt their own experience and keep them quiet. Some other ways gaslighting sounds are:

- *"You* threw yourself at *me*—everybody saw it!"

- "You wanted it."

- "You said you wanted help/for me to come in."

- "You came to my room. What did you expect?"

- "You made me hit/yell at/etc. you. If only you didn't do [such and such], I wouldn't have . . ."

- "You were so into it! I'm glad you had such a good time."

Sometimes the attacker uses threats to prevent the victim-survivor from breaking their silence, for example, "If you tell, I'll . . .

- . . . hurt you or someone you care about."

- . . . out you [as queer or trans, as undocumented, etc.]."

- . . . get you deported."

- . . . share naked photos of you."

- . . . make sure you lose custody of the kids."

- . . . tell everyone about what you did."

- . . . make your life a living hell."

Abusive partners can use any of these types of follow-up, and some kinds of approaches are designed specifically to keep you in a relationship, like:

- "You're the only one who understands me."

- "No one else would want you."

- "I'm really sorry. I promise I'll never do that again. Please forgive me."

- "I can't live without you. If you leave, I'll hurt [or kill] myself."

Aggressors also can use these lines in the testing and isolating stages to get past our boundaries or other efforts to be safe.

WHAT THEY SAW. Look at the stories in Chapter 2. What factors do you think the aggressors used in selecting the people to target? In a notebook, write those down, along with any notes about what approach and tests they used. If you'd like, answer these questions while thinking about your own situation. Identifying how aggressors operate can help you recognize it if it happens in real life.

PART 2

Ploys, Parting Shots, and Other Red Flags

Ploys and parting shots are ways harassers, abusers, and attackers move us through the stages of assault. They're strategies aggressors use to gain access to us, to control us and the situation, and to overcome any resistance we put up. We'll describe each one in more detail to help you know them when you see them.

PLOYS

Ploys are tricks and manipulations harassers, abusers, and attackers use to get what they want. They use ploys to get access to someone, isolate them, or involve them in a relationship. They use ploys to maintain control, whether that means keeping someone in a relationship or keeping them from speaking up about what happened. Here are some of the most common.

QUESTIONS, AKA THE CONVERSATION WEB

Asking questions and engaging someone in conversation may seem innocent. But during the (usually unwanted) conversation, the aggressor asks questions that steer the direction and content of the conversation, pressuring us to go along with them—and so they establish control.

When doing this, they're also getting information about our lives and about how we respond when threatened, controlled, or manipulated.

Although they seem harmless at first, these conversations can easily become problematic. With someone we don't know, they can slide into things like

"Where do you live? You live alone?" "Are you seeing someone? Why not? A beautiful being like you?" We get into a pattern of answering, and before we know it, we've given out way more info than we feel comfortable with. With someone we do know, the conversation web can show up in ways like "You're bisexual? What's better, sex with a woman or a man? You must love three-somes!" or "Your boyfriend lets you come here without him?"

A question asker is in a power position, as the person answering isn't only giving information but is put in a position of reacting. Lying and being evasive can backfire, ensnaring us in the web. For example, if you say, "I have AIDS," the aggressor might say, "That's okay, I do too," or "I'll wear a condom." If you say, "My partner will be home soon," the aggressor might say, "That's okay. When I hear their car, I'll leave."

"Why are you asking me that?" is a wonderful response to questions and restores some of your power. So does asking questions of them, telling them you don't want to talk, or just being done with the conversation.

Teresa's Story
Out in the wilderness

Teresa was volunteering for the forest service at a remote lake. She stayed at a tiny, isolated campground. One day, a member of the public engaged her in friendly conversation, and he eventually asked if she stayed there overnight. Taught to be polite to the public, Teresa told him she did. When he asked where she stayed, she waved in the general direction of the campground and said, "Over there." He then asked, "Do you stay alone?" Teresa was getting uncom-fortable, so she lied and said "no." He then asked whether the other people there were all women. At that point she was so terrified that she commuted for the rest of the summer rather than stay at the lake.

REQUESTS FOR HELP

Requests for help can especially affect those of us raised female, as we're trained to be nurturers and caretakers. Saying "no" to someone who needs help can make us feel guilty, and an aggressor may take advantage of that. Do any of these sound familiar?

- "I've had an awful day/I'm really freaked out. I need you to come over and talk."

- "Will you help me give my cat a pill? They have to have it tonight but it's really a two-person job."

- "Can you show me the way to the subway? My phone battery ran out and I can't find it."

When you think the request is legit, another option is to think of a way to help that doesn't put you in jeopardy, which might be getting help *for* them or brainstorming solutions with them. Often you can find someone better equipped to step up while keeping yourself safe.

OFFERS OF HELP

If someone offers to help us—or actually does help us—we may feel we owe them. We may feel ungrateful if we respond to a request or suggestion with mistrust or by refusing. The same is true if someone does us a favor or spends money on us, and then acts as if we owe them something (um, sex?). We may feel guilty or indebted, leading us to do things we don't really want to do.

FLATTERY

Flattery can be about physical appearance, abilities, or other characteristics. It may be used to persuade us to participate in modeling sessions, in "special" or private work with teachers, mentors, or coaches, and in other interactions where the aggressor gets us alone.

It may be difficult to resist flattery when we need to feel affirmed, recognized, or accepted, especially if we're feeling low or don't have enough connection in our life. At first it might seem fine, and we like the attention. We usually get uncomfortable later on, but telling others what's happening gets harder at that point because we often blame ourselves for accepting the extra attention.

PRESSURE FROM AUTHORITY

People with power that comes with the role they fill—police, teachers, doctors, coaches, immigration officials, and faith leaders, for example—may use their expertise or positions of authority to intimidate us or get us to trust them. Others may pretend to be authority figures to get our trust. Either way, they then abuse that trust.

IT'S AN EMERGENCY!

Aggressors sometimes pressure us by claiming there's an emergency such as an injured person, a family member stranded or in the hospital, a child being kidnapped, or a gas leak. The goal is to get us to open the door, to go with them, or to do something else we wouldn't normally do. The combination of urgency and authority may effectively pressure us to ignore caution (and our intuition) or to rush to action without thinking the situation through.

Let me in. I haven't got all day. Your landlord's going to be royally pissed if you don't let me fix the leak right now.

INTIMIDATION AND PUT-DOWNS

Intimidation can show up as anything from an impatient tone to straight-up threats. Put-downs damage our sense of self and confidence in our perceptions, making us more susceptible to boundary crossing. "If you weren't such a bitch/prude . . ." "If you weren't so ugly/fat . . ." "If you weren't so uptight . . ." "C'mon, you said you liked [this sexual thing]. You're a slut and everyone knows it." In addition to intimidating us, such manipulations can lead us to comply because we want to prove the aggressor wrong about us.

DIVIDE AND CONQUER

If two or more people are being targeted and one responds to the aggressor's approach in a strong, negative way, the aggressor might turn to the other person and say something like "Your friend isn't very nice, huh? They think they're too good for me? I can tell you aren't like that." As with intimidation and put-downs, this also may pressure the more cautious person to abandon their boundary to prove the aggressor wrong.

APOLOGIES, PROMISES, AND REASSURANCE

After offending us or arousing our suspicions, an aggressor may apologize a lot and promise us that whatever they did won't ever happen again. Apologies often are along the lines of: "I'm so sorry. I know better than that, but I just wanted to get to know you so badly. Forgive me?"

In using this ploy, aggressors may tell us just what we'd like to hear. Once they have our trust back, they move in again: "I'd never hurt you. You can trust me." They may even do it before we feel suspicious, saying something like "Don't worry, I'm not the type who puts my hands on people without permission."

STOPPING BY HOME

When we're getting a ride, the driver may say they need to stop somewhere to pick something up (like their wallet or phone) or to check on someone. Once there, they invite us in "for just a minute" and begin a physical assault.

HELP WITH THE KIDS

This person makes friends with our children and seems to have endless energy for them. Sometimes they're grooming a child for abuse, and sometimes they're doing this as a way to get to us. If we're single parents or have a heavy parenting load for other reasons (for example, a partner who's stationed abroad or a child with lots of medical needs), we might be more susceptible to this tactic.

WE'RE ALL HERE TO HAVE FUN

Some aggressors take advantage of the open atmosphere of situations like concerts, festivals, and parties to cross people's boundaries. If we object, we're called a mood killer or accused of ruining the fun, pressuring us to ignore our boundaries and go along.

THE ANSWER TO YOUR PROBLEMS

This person has the answer to all our problems and is ready to fix them. It could be a place to stay, help paying bills, or something else. Sometimes they offer to protect us from a difficult family member, friend, or boss. Especially when they're a romantic or sex partner, this gives them enormous power over us.

This list of ploys DOESN'T MEAN that you shouldn't ever help someone, take a compliment, have a conversation, believe an apology, or accept help. Rather, the list is here to BOOST YOUR AWARENESS of common ploys so that if your intuition tells you something's WRONG, you're more likely to TRUST it.

(See Chapter 5 for more on connecting with your intuition.)

FIND THE PLOYS. Take a look at the stories in Chapter 2. Were there signs that something wasn't right? (Signs that something isn't right can include how the person being targeted feels.) What did the aggressors do, say, or use to get what they wanted? Note any ploys you see in each story.

What other ploys or manipulations have you seen in your life? It doesn't have to be something that happened to you; it could be something a friend or family member told you about or something you saw on a TV show or social media. Write them below.

Next, write the ploys, dynamics, or comments most likely to get to you. Knowing what they are can help you resist them. What are some other things you could do in a stressful or threatening situation so you don't fall for a ploy? Write them here too. (Remember, when we say "write," we don't necessarily mean *write*. You can draw, doodle, tell a friend, record it on your phone, or do whatever works for you.)

PARTING SHOTS

Another way harassers, abusers, and attackers manipulate is with a parting shot. Knowing what a parting shot is will help you stay strong in the face of one.

When someone's manipulating us, they're likely to react to our assertiveness or other efforts to be safe by saying something designed to make us feel guilty, uncertain, bad, unworthy, unattractive, threatened, or some other difficult emotion. These statements may be a last-ditch attempt to get us to go along with them (in which case, they're used as a ploy), a way to keep us from talking about what they did, or a way for them to save face as they give up and leave us alone. Many are similar to the follow-up after an assault.

Some common parting shots in response to a boundary:

- "No wonder people say you're cruel/cold/selfish/uptight . . ."

- "I'd *never* hurt you. How could you think I'd be that kind of person?"

- "Don't flatter yourself. You think I'd even be into you?"

- "Why are you so sensitive? You overreact to everything."

- "I can't believe you won't help me. What's this world coming to when you can't even get some help?"

- "What would the boss think if they knew you're so uncooperative?"

- "You just hate White people!"

- "How *dare* you suggest I was trying to harass you."

- "I'm just trying to be friendly. So no one's allowed to be friendly anymore?"

- "BITCH!"

When faced with a parting shot, resist the urge to deny, argue, or respond. Instead, you can choose not to respond, or you can agree and reframe it. For example, you might say or think, "You bet I'm a bitch. And proud of it," or "Sure, and I'm just getting started." If you start explaining yourself, you're still in the interaction and are open to more manipulation. Knowing that an aggressor is likely to use a parting shot can protect us from damage to our self-esteem and avoid kicking up self-doubt.

The only people who get upset when you start setting boundaries are the ones who benefited from you not having them.

Even someone who'll later think about what you said and become more thoughtful or respectful is likely to be defensive at first. Someone who wasn't intending to majorly cross your boundaries will probably be offended that you thought they might.

But we have a right to expect aggressors, most of whom are cis men, to become more aware of what life is like for those of us most often targeted for gender-based violence. You might get a reaction that tells you your boundary was well received. Some examples are, "I'm really sorry. I guess that was pretty insensitive," "Wow, I didn't realize I was being pushy. I didn't mean to bother you," or "I didn't think about it that way. Do you really think that kind of joke is a problem?"

Although apologies can be manipulation to get back in, it's also possible that someone learned from your boundary!

When this happens, thank them, take it in, and praise yourself for a job well done. Then take some time to think about whether you can trust them enough to engage with them in the future. An apology doesn't mean you have to change your boundary.

MAKE IT PERSONAL—PARTING SHOTS. What parting shots have you heard? What parting shots do you fear hearing? It doesn't have to be something that happened to you; it could be something a friend or family member told you about or something you saw on a TV show or on social media.

In a notebook, or in the chart on the next page, write them down, along with the parting shots most likely to get to you. Knowing them will help you resist them if you encounter them in real life. Knowing what gets to you can help you be ready for statements that might be hurtful, get past your boundaries, or cause you to abandon your own needs.

TROUBLESHOOTING. You've noted some ploys and parting shots likely to get to you. Choose one and write something you can say to yourself (or to the other person) to help you hold your boundary.

For example, a ploy that might feel difficult to deal with is someone saying you owe them something (like sex or a date) after they did you a favor. Imagine the details of such a situation. Maybe the person gave you a ride, brought you groceries, got you concert tickets, or shared their Netflix password.

What you might say to yourself: "I deserve a favor without owing payment." (This is a kind of affirmation that reinforces your right to your feelings and your boundaries. We'll talk more about affirmations in Chapter 6.)

What you might say to them: "I appreciate your help. But if you expected something in return for helping me, you needed to make that clear before."

PLOY

To myself:

_____

To them:

_____

To myself:

_____

To them:

_____

PARTING SHOT

To myself:

_____

To them:

_____

To myself:

_____

To them:

Nadia's Story
The study date

I was new on campus and invited to a study date. Being a serious student and naive, I took the invite literally. But when I got there, it was clear that the guy who invited me was ready to party and wanted me to "put out" sexually. I did manage to set a boundary. He backed off, but not before quoting poetry about how women are teases. I was safe, but I ended up depressed for days.

RED FLAGS

Aggressors do other things that signal danger, and when they do, there's good reason to be cautious. Unfortunately, it can be difficult to see these danger signals when we most need to—for example, because we like the attention or the help, or especially if we're in love.

Some red flags include someone who:

- Seems too good to be true

- Doesn't take responsibility for anything, always blaming others for the problems in their life

- Demands that you explain why you said "no" to something and keeps the focus on you and what's wrong with you

- Is obsessive, controlling, or jealous and tells you these behaviors are a sign of love. This may look like wanting to know where you are or who you're with all the time, or telling you that you shouldn't hang out with your friends or family. They also may text you constantly, want to look at your phone, or demand your passwords.

- Moves the relationship very fast. For example, they may want to have sex, be exclusive (get you to sign off of dating apps), move in together, get married, or share money before you're ready. They might use love bombing (manipulating you with excessive flattery or affection).

- Violates a personal boundary, even about something small-ish like not wanting a drink or asking them not to tag you in a picture. They may move too close, ask or say something inappropriate (often something extremely personal), or touch you without being invited or without checking first. Even if you want to be sexual with them, they may do sexual things you're not into. If you say what's okay with you and what's not around sex, they may pressure you to do things you don't want to—or just do them without your consent.

- Doesn't introduce you to their friends or family after you've been together a while.

If you set a limit and the other person doesn't respect it, that's the biggest of all red flags.

No Drink, Thanks

Jennifer Peepas, who doles out advice as Captain Awkward, summed up many of these dynamics when she wrote this:

Imagine you're at a party. A guy offers you a drink. You say no. He says "Come on, one drink!" You say "no thanks." Later, he brings you a soda. "I know you said you didn't want a drink, but I was getting one for myself and you looked thirsty." For you to refuse at this point makes you the asshole. He's just being nice, right? Predators use the social contract and our own good hearts and fear of being rude against us. If you drink the drink, you're teaching him that it just takes a little persistence on his part to overcome your "no." If you say "Really, I appreciate it, but no thanks" and put the drink down and walk away from it, you're the one who looks rude in that moment. But the fact is, you didn't ask for the drink and you don't want the drink and you don't have to drink it just to make some guy feel validated.

MAKE IT PERSONAL—RED FLAGS. Look at the stories from Chapter 2. What did the aggressors do, say, or use to get what they wanted? Note the red flags you see in each story. What other red flags have you seen in your life? It doesn't have to be something that happened to you; it could be something a friend or family member told you about or something you saw on a TV show or on social media. Write them below. Write down something you could say or do in response to a red flag.

_____

_____

_____

_____

TL;DR

- Knowing the stages of most assaults—select, approach and test, isolate, assault, and follow-up—and how they usually occur can help you recognize what's happening and interrupt it.

- Ploys, parting shots, and other red flags are ways harassers, abusers, and attackers move us through the stages of assault. Knowing them can help us recognize them and stay safer.

- With the tools included here, you can bolster your strengths for resisting these manipulations and abuses of power.

THE HEART OF THE MATTER. *What's the best thing (maybe two or three things, since there was a lot) you're going to remember from this chapter? Do you feel more ready to deal with ploys, parting shots, or other red flags? You don't have to answer these exact questions, but please do note your takeaways.*

SELF-CARE BREAK. *Take a deep breath. What self-care will you do now that you've finished this chapter? It can be a small thing (like a few seconds of stretching) or something bigger (like a day off). For more ideas, check in with the plan you made on page xix or the ideas we list on page 10.*

YOU ALWAYS DID THE BEST YOU COULD! *We know it, and we hope you do too. Join us in celebrating whatever you've done to get through. Now that you know more, you'll have more options. This is cliché but true: knowledge is power.*

"TRAUMA IN A **PERSON,**
DECONTEXTUALIZED
OVER TIME, LOOKS LIKE
PERSONALITY.
TRAUMA IN A **FAMILY,**
DECONTEXTUALIZED
OVER TIME, LOOKS LIKE
TRAITS.

TRAUMA IN A **PEOPLE,**
DECONTEXTUALIZED
OVER TIME, LOOKS LIKE
CULTURE."

—Resmaa Menakem

Chapter 4

IS THERE SOMETHING WRONG WITH ME?

Hint: It's Not Your Fault

GROUNDING & CENTERING: Be a friend to yourself. Take a deep breath. Think about something stressful or challenging going on in your life. Say some sympathetic and reassuring phrases to yourself that you might say to a friend who's going through what you're going through. Some examples: "I'm here for you." "I care about you." "I'm sorry about what you're going through." If you find one phrase that feels right, repeat it a few times. Close with another deep breath.

Sexist and racist violence are supported by rape culture. Rape culture includes denying how common sexual violence is, blaming those targeted, and conditioning women and LGBTQIA+ people to be victims of that violence. In this chapter, we'll look at the role of culture and our internal barriers to change, and where they both come from. (Later, we'll explore how to change them.)

PART 1

Social Forces

So many people believe that their inability to speak up for themselves as often or as effectively as they'd like is a personal shortcoming. But really, culture, family, school, religion, and other social institutions train us to be that way. As the chapter title says, it's not your fault. In this chapter, we'll look at how we were trained to relate to boundary violations, starting with the big picture: patriarchy.

Patriarchal cultures refuse to see the full range of gender-based violence and how common it is. They also ignore violence based on other forms of oppression, such as racism and ableism. By pretending that violence is rare and that only a few "deviant," "perverted," "mentally ill," or "abnormal" individuals carry it out, people don't have to take responsibility for the ways society allows and promotes mistreatment.

When society denies the violence that happens to us, we trust ourselves and our realities less, and that makes us more vulnerable. Myths, stereotypes, and a complicated set of misunderstandings about rape and other forms of violence protect those responsible and put the focus on blaming and controlling those who are targeted.

These myths include beliefs like "Lesbians just need to have sex with the right man," "Disabled people are lucky if anyone wants to have sex with them," and "Children and people with intellectual disabilities don't understand what's happening to them, so 'sex' with them isn't a big deal."

It's hard to trust your own perceptions when those around you are saying you're wrong. People minimize the amount and severity of gender-based violence, and often it's dismissed as a "he said–she said" situation. (What other violence is treated that way?)

For example, despite how widespread partner abuse and sexual assault are, we're judged for taking steps to protect ourselves—or for not doing what people think we should be doing to protect ourselves. We're told we're overreacting and being "too sensitive," being paranoid, or even lying.

Social expectations put women in particular in a position where we can't win: We're wrong if we *do* speak up ("You're a bitch/people won't like you if you act that way/if you tell the truth you'll ruin my life.") and we're wrong if we *don't* speak up ("Why didn't you say something/tell them to stop/fight back/leave?"). We're told we have something to gain (Money? Fame? Ha!) from making accusations, aka telling the truth about our lives. Meanwhile, the violence continues, and it maintains sexism and other oppressions by keeping us fearful, dependent on others for protection, and limited in what we feel we can safely do.

VICTIM-BLAMING

Victim-blaming is the tendency to examine the target's behavior—rather than the aggressor's—to see what "caused" the harassment, abuse, or assault.

Victim-blaming shows up in questions like:

- "What were you wearing?"

- "Did you know the attacker?"

- "Why do/did you stay with them?"

- "Why did you get so drunk?"

- "Why did you go to that party/that neighborhood/that person's house?"

- "What did you expect, going up to their room?"

- "Why didn't you say something/fight back/leave?"

- "Why did you stay in touch with the attacker?"

Victim-blaming also shows up in news coverage that talks about the victim-survivor's behavior and in court cases where a victim-survivor's sexual history is discussed.

This perspective is so normal that we may not notice that we've barely paid any attention to the aggressor and their behavior. This is a double standard.

Think of the role of alcohol in sexual assault. (FYI, alcohol is involved in half of all sexual assaults.) In heterosexual rapes, drinking convicts the woman

("She should have known better than to get drunk") and exonerates the man ("He didn't know what he was doing, he was drunk").

To keep the system of power going, society and individuals blame those with less power for their own suffering. When we internalize the blame—when we believe we're to blame because others say we are—we keep the focus off the aggressors, and in doing so, we remove any pressure for them to stop. This dynamic often creates hostility among oppressed groups, again diverting the attention from those creating the conditions for the violence to happen. Victim-blaming and self-blame reinforce power imbalances and enable gender-based violence to keep happening.

But we know that if you're harassed, abused, or attacked, the responsibility lies entirely (100%, totally, completely, in every way) with the person who did it. And it's important that you know that too.

For individuals, the consequences of victim-blaming can be devastating. The response a survivor gets from the first people they tell after a sexual assault affects their ability to recover and heal. Empathetic, validating, loving support helps people recover from all kinds of trauma, including interpersonal violence.

Unfortunately, women often participate in victim-blaming. Just one example: the women who came to Donald Trump's defense (most of them White)—and voted for him!—after his "Grab them by the pussy" comments became public. Those who are targeted for gender-based violence (mostly women and LGBTQIA+ people) often blame survivors in order to reassure ourselves that we're safe and to give ourselves a sense of control. We think things like "They shouldn't have gotten that drunk. I never let myself black out because that's basically an invitation for someone to rape you."

Recognize this for what it is: an attempt to construct a false sense of security at the victim's expense.

And some women participate in the blaming to stay in the favor of the men involved; to become allies with those who have the power. Women who stand up for other women often risk the wrath—and rejection—of their social group.

The victim-blaming functions as a way to control our behavior. Women are divided into "good" and "bad." Only "bad girls" get raped, the myth goes; if you "behave," you won't get attacked. This, of course, isn't true.

Assault is assault, whether you're at home, at a party, or doing your job (yes, even if you're a sex worker). Until we hold aggressors responsible for their actions, violence won't decrease.

Asking for It?

To show why most sexual assault survivors choose not to press charges, law student Connie K. Borkenhagen asks us, in an article in the *American Bar Association Journal*, to imagine someone who's been robbed undergoing the same sort of interrogation as someone who's been raped:

"Mr. Smith, you were held up at gunpoint on the corner of First and Main?"

"Yes."

"Did you struggle with the robber?"

"No."

"Why not?"

"He was armed."

"Then you made a conscious decision to comply with his demands rather than resist?"

"Yes."

"Did you scream? Cry out?"

"No. I was afraid."

"I see. Have you ever been held up before?"

"No."

"Have you ever given money away?"

"Yes, of course."

"And you did so willingly?"

"What are you getting at?"

"Well, let's put it like this, Mr. Smith. You've given money away in the past. In fact, you have quite a reputation for philanthropy. How can we be sure you weren't contriving to have your money taken by force?"

"Listen, if I wanted..."

"Never mind. What time did this holdup take place?"

"About 11 p.m."

"You were out on the street at 11 p.m.? Doing what?"

"Just walking."

"Just walking? You know that it's dangerous being out on the street that late at night. Weren't you aware that you could have been held up?"

"I hadn't thought about it."

"What were you wearing?"

"Let's see—a suit. Yes, a suit."

"An expensive suit?"

"Well—yes. I'm a successful lawyer, you know."

"In other words, Mr. Smith, you were walking around the streets late at night in a suit that practically advertised the fact that you might be a good target for some easy money, isn't that so? I mean, if we didn't know better, Mr. Smith, we might even think you were asking for this to happen, mightn't we?"

PART 2

Our Internal Barriers

All these social forces set up many of us from an early age to be victimized. We've been encouraged to behave in ways that work against us, and we've often been discouraged from developing traits needed for resistance. This creates barriers to self-defense.

Barriers to Self-Defense

- Denial
- Passivity
- Self-blame
- Feelings of low self-worth

Sometimes there are things we might have done to keep ourselves safer but we couldn't. Maybe we didn't know about the actions we could have taken. Maybe our conditioning stopped us. Maybe we froze when confronted with a threat. (Freezing is a real thing and it's a survival mechanism, so don't get down on it!) And don't forget all the things you *have* done to increase your safety! (We'll get to that in a minute.)

When we've been aware of what to do but were unable to do it, we often feel worse than in situations where there weren't any clear options.

We'll look at each behavior and belief in more detail, aspiring to be compassionate toward—not judgmental of—ourselves.

DENIAL

Denial usually sounds something like this: "Nothing will happen to me," "They don't mean anything by it," or "It's not that bad."

Denial takes at least two forms: we may deny that something is wrong or we may deny that it hurts or bothers us (or we tell ourselves that it shouldn't bother us).

Denial does serve some functions:

- It allows us to believe that people are generally good and trustworthy.

- It keeps us from having to deal with an uncomfortable or dangerous situation. Once we fully take in the fact that something bad is happening, we have to face our fear or discomfort, abandon passivity, and decide what to do.

- It keeps us from feeling exhausted and angry. If we were aware of every single possibly problematic situation that came up and had to decide how to respond, we'd probably have no energy or goodwill left.

- If we're being abused, denial can also protect us from despair and help us to survive mentally and emotionally. It can help us psychically survive abuse at the hands of people we trust or rely on.

- It protects us from the reactions of others. If we told people what's going on, some of them might blame us or deny or minimize our experience, compounding our pain.

- Finally, it helps us avoid the possibility of being wrong, hurting someone's feelings, or looking foolish.

The problem with denial, though, is that until we recognize a problem, we can't do anything about it. We've been trained to accept our lack of choices. Becoming aware of denial is an important first step in gaining skills for well-being and safety.

Awareness allows us to see options, whether that means developing a safety plan to leave an abusive relationship, ending a conversation with someone who's crossing our boundaries, or anything else that supports our safety and well-being.

On a bigger level, we as a society can't do anything about gender-based violence until we're willing to recognize that it's a problem, it's not rare, and it's not committed by a few "abnormal" individuals. It's an issue we all have a responsibility to address.

FOLLOW THE CLUES. In the situation you've been working with in this book, were there clues that something was wrong? If so, what were they? In what ways did you pick up on them, deny them, or distrust your perceptions? If you used denial, how do you think that helped you?

_____

_____

_____

_____

_____

PASSIVITY

Passivity shows up in thoughts like these: "What will they do to me?" "What will they think of me?" or "There's nothing I can do about it." Passivity leads to giving up your own power and your own rights.

Being passive means letting others run the show. It means waiting for them to do something and then figuring out how to respond. It means acting based on what we'll tolerate ("This is my limit—if they cross it, *then* I'll say something") instead of what we want. Being passive is a sign that we feel powerless and don't believe in our ability to be effective or to get what we want.

Changing passivity doesn't mean resisting every time; it means making decisions about the best action possible in each situation. Sometimes you might stay active simply within your head and heart—for example, deciding to go along with what a mugger wants in the face of a weapon. (We call that *strategic compliance*; it's *not* passive.)

In a relationship with a violent partner, what looks like passivity might really be de-escalating in the moment and making plans to be safer in the future instead of speaking up in the moment, because the abuser may use your speaking up as an excuse for more violence. These are active choices you're making for your safety. (For more on de-escalation, see page 208.)

Sometimes we don't speak up to avoid embarrassing the person who's crossing our boundaries. They know when we're not willing to say anything, and they often exploit that to keep going or escalate their behavior.

WHAT ABOUT ME? In the situation you wrote about in Chapter 2 or another one you'd like to work with, what did you feel, need, and want? Were you able to say those things or take action on them? If you did, what made you able to? If you didn't, what got in your way?

_____

_____

_____

_____

_____

_____

_____

FAN THE FLAMES 1. Think of other times when you've responded actively to harassment, abuse, assault, or other boundary crossing, no matter how small.

What were the consequences of not being passive? Did anyone respond positively? How did it feel to you, internally, to set a limit or ask for what you wanted?

In the space below or in a journal, write about the times you set a boundary or asked for what you wanted. Throughout this book, we're going to fan those flames.

_____

_____

_____

_____

_____

Lauren's Story
Feeling helpless

I grew up in a big city where street harassment, starting for me when I was eleven, was a constant reminder of the threat of rape. I always believed that if anyone ever tried to rape me, there'd be nothing I could do—because I assumed they'd be bigger and stronger than I was.

When I was twenty-eight, I took my first self-defense class and learned that I did have options, and I did have power. But until then, the belief in my own powerlessness pretty much immobilized me.

Society tells women especially that we can't successfully protect or defend ourselves. Like Lauren, we come to believe that we can't possibly stop an assault. What's particularly harmful is the message that any kind of resistance will make an attacker "angrier," so we should do nothing. So many things are wrong with this message, including the fact that research shows that those who resist sexual assault are very often successful, and that even if they are raped, those who resist don't sustain significantly more injuries than those who do not.

SELF-BLAME

Regret ≠ blame

We've talked about how common self-blame is. "Why didn't I run?" "I didn't say 'no,'" "I shouldn't have agreed to see them again," and "I should have said something sooner" are self-blaming thoughts. While we may have regrets about what we did or didn't do ("I wish I hadn't gone to their room"), that doesn't mean we're responsible for the harm done to us. If we think, "It's my fault, because I went to their room," that's self-blame that society has taught us.

Most of us who are survivors know in our rational minds that we're not responsible for what someone does to us, but it's much harder to hold that in our hearts. Still, because societies and cultures tend to blame victims, it's common for us to feel responsible for (and guilty about) what's been done to us. In this way, we're victimized twice. And if friends, family, or authorities also tell us we're responsible, we're victimized a third time.

It's easy to blame ourselves for the times when we haven't been able to protect ourselves. But it's not our fault. It's the fault of a society and a culture that teach us that other people—and what they think of us—are more important than we are and that we shouldn't be angry or have needs. This is more of the damage patriarchy does to us.

If we're filled with shame and self-blame, we're unlikely to talk about what happened (or is happening), and we're unlikely to turn our energy or anger outward to the person harming us or the society that accepts harassment, abuse, and assault.

Self-blame can also be a way to keep ourselves from feeling powerless. If we believe that we were in some way responsible for the harassment, abuse, or attack, then we had at least some control over the situation and can, theoretically, avoid future problems if we do something different. What's more, people with multiple marginalized identities often are expected to behave as a representative of their entire group, and those expectations can intensify self-blame.

To counter self-blame, we need to get in touch with our anger at what was done to us—and women's anger generally isn't encouraged or allowed.

TO SPEAK OR NOT TO SPEAK. In the situation you wrote about in Chapter 2, or another one from your life, did you share what happened with others? If you didn't, what were the reasons you decided not to?

If you did share your experience, how did people respond? Did their responses contribute to feelings of shame, self-blame, or denial? Did their responses help you feel compassion for yourself or anger at the aggressor?

_____

_____

_____

_____

WHO TAKES THE BLAME? What did you tell yourself about who was responsible for the harassment, abuse, or assault done to you? Was there anything you wanted from an interaction that may have added to self-blame? (For example, maybe you wanted them to like you, or you were afraid of hurting their feelings.)

_____

_____

_____

_____

I'M ALLOWED TO. We may have regrets about something we did or didn't do. It can be difficult to acknowledge those regrets without blaming ourselves for what happened, but it's important to do so.

Fill in the blanks below. We've put some ideas in parentheses, but feel free to use your own words:

I'm allowed to _____ (want attention, take a risk, get drunk, be naive, flirt, hook up, change my mind).

That doesn't cause or justify _____ (harassment, abuse, or assault), and it's no excuse for it.

WHEN I SPOKE UP. If you set a boundary with the person who harassed, abused, or attacked you, did they say or do anything that added to your feelings of self-blame? (If you didn't confront them, what do you imagine they might have said?)

_____

_____

_____

We're not saying you should confront an aggressor. That choice is always yours, and you're free to make it and to change your mind at any time.

Sometimes boundary setting may not be the safest option. That's often true in a relationship with someone who's abusing you. Sometimes the best thing to do is to protect ourselves internally, reminding ourselves of our basic goodness, strength, and right to be safe, while recognizing that what the abuser is doing is wrong and making plans to be safer in the future.

FEELINGS OF LOW SELF-WORTH

We live in a world that devalues anyone who isn't White, cis, able-bodied, and male.

All forms of oppression cause feelings of low self-worth. Racism, classism, ableism, religious oppression, and the rest tell us that we have less value than the dominant group. One result is that we place other people's feelings and opinions above our own, and we spend too much time and energy trying to fit in or not be othered.

Low self-worth can also result from child abuse (sexual, physical, or emotional) or alcoholic or other types of dysfunctional families. These experiences can create an overwhelming need for approval, a fear of criticism, or a sense that everything's our fault. Feelings of low self-worth can make it difficult to trust our perceptions or to believe that our feelings or needs count. This is especially true if someone disagrees with our perceptions, feelings, or needs.

Many of us are conditioned to believe that others are more important than we are. We're taught to put others—and their feelings—first and to value their opinions more than our own.

"That's okay, it doesn't matter" and "Their feelings matter more" are the kinds of things you might think if you have feelings of low self-worth. We focus on the other person's wants and needs without expecting them to care about ours.

It can be difficult to believe our feelings and needs matter. In the thrift store, Nadia was worried about how the staff member would feel if she spoke up, but she didn't ask herself if he cared about her feelings or the fact that his actions were making her uncomfortable.

And more than that, even though the world is dangerous for us, we often require that we be 100% right about what's happening (and be sure of the aggressor's intentions) before taking action to protect ourselves. We may worry so much about the possibility of hurting someone's feelings (or being seen as aggressive or not being liked) that we don't speak or act, even when the consequences can be serious. These fears prevent us from clearly seeing the risk or our options.

We may give the other person the benefit of the doubt, often even when we know that they don't respect our needs or wishes or that they're actually dangerous. We may have a double standard, making allowances for others' (especially men's) behavior in ways we don't make for our own. We may worry about whether they like or approve of us, never asking ourselves if we like or approve of them.

Our sense of self-worth becomes connected to their opinion of us rather than our own opinion of ourselves.

This conditioning's so deep that even when physical self-defense seems the best option, we may be reluctant to hurt someone—despite their clear willingness to hurt us. We're taught that women are somehow superior for a common reluctance to use physical force, even though that reluctance is rarely a choice. Instead, that reluctance usually comes from the belief that our use of force wouldn't be effective.

Tellingly, we're often willing to have someone else use violence to protect us—or use it ourselves in order to protect someone else (like a child), even though we can't imagine using it to protect ourselves.

WHO CAME FIRST? Looking at your own experience from Chapter 2, write the ways you put the other person's needs first or gave them the benefit of the doubt. If you were concerned about their liking or approving of you, write that down too.

_____

_____

_____

_____

FIND THE NEGATIVE SELF-TALK. Pick a couple of stories from the examples in Chapter 2. Note where in each story denial, passivity, self-blame, or feelings of low self-worth played a role. Then do the same with one of your own experiences.

_____

_____

_____

_____

_____

PART 3

Where the Barriers Come From

GENDER ROLES

To develop compassion for ourselves and to begin to transform the ways we've been trained not to resist, it's helpful to understand where denial, passivity, self-blame, and feelings of low self-worth come from. While what's considered feminine does vary from culture to culture, in most cultures, women are expected to defer to men. Women are valued for being self-sacrificing and nurturing. We're taught that much (or most) of our value is in how we look. Many of us learn at an early age to be passive, to put other people's needs before our own, to doubt our own judgment, and more.

Too often in the dominant U.S. culture (White and middle-class), the message from books, movies, TV shows, and school is that being female means being sweet, nice, quiet, trusting, friendly, helpful, caring, passive, helpless, indirect, thin, pretty, and dependent. (The reward supposedly is that Prince Charming will swoop in and complete us! And then we'll live happily ever after?)

Our caregivers told us, directly or not, what the rules of being a "nice girl," a "good woman," or a "lady" were. We were trained to care about other people's feelings and often to put their needs first. Our caregivers probably thought these traits would help keep us safe, allow us to fit in, make us more lovable. And even if our caregivers *didn't* enforce these rules, at least some of our friends, acquaintances, and the larger society probably did.

Women still do the vast majority of the cleaning, cooking, and childcare; states are pushing through anti-LGBTQIA+, especially anti-trans, legislation; bodily autonomy and reproductive rights are being demolished; and during the pandemic, women (especially women of color) were pushed out of jobs at much higher rates than men were, showing that women's contribution to the workforce is still less valued.

> No, dear, girls shouldn't fight.

Many people raised female were taught to be afraid of standing up for ourselves and to mostly rely on others. We're not always given the tools to take charge of a situation, speak up assertively, demand respect, have confidence in our abilities, or feel worthy of defense. This deprives us of the survival skills we need in order to avoid and deal with the violence in our lives.

The roles we learn aren't the same for every race or economic class. Some of the characteristics seen as ideal for women and femmes require privilege to obtain and carry out. Girls raised with cultural norms outside the dominant White and middle class (for example, BIPOC girls or low-income White girls) may be brought up with some of these qualities as well as some that can also make keeping themselves safe difficult. For example, Black girls may be taught to stick up for themselves and told that

> Why didn't you fight back?

no one else will stick up for them, even as they're portrayed as more adult and as threatening, and even as they're sometimes punished (within and outside the Black community) for sticking up for themselves. Black women are also discouraged from discussing Black men's violence against them, for fear of being seen as "race traitors." The cultural setup can vary, but the result is that we're targeted for gender-based violence.

Women and LGBTQIA+ people from some oppressed groups are encouraged to behave in certain ways when dealing with members of groups with power over them, but are more authentically themselves with those in their own racial or ethnic group. Plus, stereotypes—such as "pushy" Jewish women, "quiet" Asian women, "strong" or "angry" Black women—affect how those women are treated by people not in their racial or ethnic group. It can also affect the way those of us in these categories see ourselves and cause us to try to avoid behaviors that conform to the stereotypes.

Men and boys are taught that they must be strong—and that the way to be powerful is to have power over others. They are pushed into aggressive behaviors, harming their humanity and well-being, and setting them up to treat women and LGBTQIA+ people disrespectfully and even violently.

Men who won't be violent still face powerful pressure to stay silent and not confront their peers' bad behavior. Men who are exploring more healthy masculinities are ridiculed as "beta males" by those wanting to uphold the old gender hierarchy. In these ways, a strict gender binary and rigid gender roles still have a strong hold on society, harming everyone and making many of us vulnerable. As women and LGBTQIA+ people have gained rights and influence, the backlash, especially in far-right circles, is intensifying.

Although society is now embracing more flexible and expansive gender roles, a lot of informal rules about boys and girls—who they should be, how they should behave—still exist. Growing up we learn what girls "can" and "can't" do and what girls are "good at" and "bad at." Non-binary and trans children also learn what's okay for them to do and be—and what's off-limits.

Yes, toy stores are starting to combine what used to be separate boys' and girls' aisles, more women are studying STEM, some states allow non-binary gender markers on IDs, and the women's national soccer team is finally (!) getting paid what the men's team does.

We have Malala Yousafzai, Beyoncé, Billy Porter, Greta Thunberg, Lil Nas X, the Woman King, and Ketanji Brown Jackson as role models. But change is slow.

The "ideal" feminine qualities aren't *wrong,* and some improve both our lives and the world. Some, though, help others at our expense. For example, selflessness (self-less-ness: a telling word) can be a positive trait in some circumstances. However, insisting on selflessness from femme people most of the time is very damaging. It's the fact that the female gender role includes few other acceptable options that's harmful and puts us at risk.

THE FLOWER: LEARNING TO BE A GIRL

The flower is a symbol of femininity. Cut flowers may make our world beautiful, but without roots, they don't survive long.

WHAT WAS I TAUGHT? If you're a woman or were raised female, what lessons were you taught about what it means to be "nice" or "good"? Write them in the petals of the flower on the following page. These messages about how to be a girl can vary depending on race, ethnicity, economic class, or other identities. Maybe you were told (directly or indirectly) that you need to be pretty, thin, ladylike, agreeable, or able to please a man. Think about where those messages came from.

HEALTHY MESSAGES. What messages did you get that can help you stay safe, valued, or well? Write those on the roots. For example, you may have learned to be confident, independent, outspoken, or in touch with your feelings.

THOSE WHO BREAK THE RULES. What happens to those who don't fit in or follow the rules? What kinds of names are they called? Write your answers to the left of the flower.

If you've had experiences where people judged you—or harmed you—because you didn't fit the stereotype of your gender, write what happened to you to the right of the flower.

When we change our behavior, someone will probably retaliate by calling us names, withdrawing their connection, or trying to harm us. These words and actions can be powerful pressures to get back in the flower petals and act according to the rules of our gender.

TAKING UP SPACE. When you were growing up, what ways were you encouraged to take up or give up space? Think of physical space (like body size and posture, and whether you sit with your legs together or apart, tilt your head, or stand or sit straight), keeping your eyes up, voice volume, and emotional space (being quiet or speaking up).

Were you encouraged to develop skills or to see yourself as incompetent? Did people remark on certain qualities, like being active, aware, self-loving, or angry?

Draw a circle below for each part of your life, like school, work, friends, family, hobbies, and community. Inside each circle, draw another circle that shows how much space you take up. Do you feel the amount you take up is too small, too big, or just right? Take a pen in another color and draw a circle that's the size you want to be in that part of your life.

OPPRESSION AND SELF-HATE

Oppression makes it hard for those who are oppressed to reduce the barriers to speaking up for and protecting ourselves.

The harm is compounded when we internalize it; when oppression becomes self-hate. An efficient method for maintaining the way things are is to encourage marginalized people and groups to hate themselves and each other.

Those of us in oppressed groups are taught in many ways that we aren't as good as those with more power. If we're women or queer or poor or BIPOC or fat or have a disability or chronic illness—or if we have several of these identities—we may unconsciously believe that we're less than, since that's how we're treated in the work world, schools, health-care system, media . . . pretty much everywhere.

We're discouraged from valuing our unique characteristics and cultures, and we're encouraged to seek approval from and imitate those in the dominant group in order to help us feel worthy.

For example, "thinking like a man" is considered a compliment, while "feminine intuition" is ridiculed. Sign language is considered inferior to spoken language, and D/deaf and hard of hearing people have been forcibly kept from using it in favor of lip-reading and spoken language so that they seem as much like hearing people as possible—and are thus excluded from much meaningful communication. Indigenous children were stolen from their families and sent to institutions where they were given new names and forbidden to speak their languages.

We learn to be ashamed of who we are and to be as much like those in power as possible. Sometimes we even go as far as trying to pass, hiding our true identities and fearing we'll be found out. Passing separates us from our natural allies, often including our own families or others like us.

> **Internalized oppression** is when members of an oppressed group adopt the beliefs and stereotypes about their own group that come from the dominant group. For example, dark-skinned people who use skin-lightening products, women who slut-shame other women, and LGBQA+ people who try to change their sexual orientation are all acting from internalized oppression.

Self-hate or internalized oppression grows when we're encouraged to believe that those with power have earned their positions fairly, and that there's something "natural" about our lower position on the ladder—like we must be less intelligent or less hardworking.

All of this means we not only have less power in society but also that we have less self-confidence to rely on. It's harder to find the self-love and confidence we need to protect and defend ourselves.

NEGATIVE FEEDBACK. How have you been encouraged to devalue your own identity and characteristics?

Some examples:

- As a fat person, I've been told I have "no willpower."
- As a woman, I've been told I'm "too emotional."
- As a disabled person, I've been told I'm "a burden."
- As a/an _____ , I've been told _____ .
- As a/an _____ , I've been told _____ .
- As a/an _____ , I've been told _____ .

Note any ways these messages, positive or negative, influence your ability to advocate for yourself, keep yourself safe, or protect your well-being.

_____

_____

_____

_____

MY STRENGTHS. In addition to suffering hardships, oppressed people often develop impressive strengths. Struggling to survive and to maintain dignity, we may be more likely to develop resourcefulness, determination, crisis-management skills, self- and community-reliance, and resilience. If this is true for you, write some of the strengths you've developed.

_____

_____

_____

_____

YOUR COPING MECHANISMS ARE NOT YOUR FAULT.

—Tara Brach

OUR HISTORIES

We've looked at how sexism and other systems of oppression cause harassment, abuse, and assault. Almost all of us have survived some form of violence (remember the spectrum on page 16). Abuse and other dysfunction in the families we grew up in also affect our ability to advocate for and protect ourselves. We may have witnessed or experienced abuse when we were children, whether physical, emotional, sexual, or financial. We may have been trafficked, sexually assaulted, harassed, or stalked. Any of those things could be happening now.

And those experiences—current or past—also affect our ability to advocate for ourselves. We may ignore our own needs in order to maintain peace.

If you experienced or witnessed abuse when you were young, one lesson you may have learned is that violence is normal and valid, and that the person being abused deserves it and is to blame for it.

Being frequently criticized, for example, encourages us to believe that we're worthless and that our feelings and thoughts are wrong. This makes us more vulnerable to abuse, since we learn to distrust our perceptions and intuition, and we don't believe in ourselves enough to take action. Others of us become bullies, possibly to protect ourselves from bullying adults, especially parents.

If you've grown up in a toxic or abusive family, you've developed coping mechanisms to survive it. Growing up in dysfunction can have other effects, including:

- Lack of assertiveness and difficulty saying "no"

- Chronic anger

- Perfectionist or overachiever tendencies

- Disconnection from your feelings, body, mind, or what's going on

- Cutting, eating disorders, substance abuse, or other self-harm

- Feeling like an object

- A deep sense of guilt and responsibility and an overwillingness to accept blame

- A failure to protect or take care of ourselves to the extent we could

- A tendency to excuse or protect aggressors

- Sexual numbness

- A belief that love is associated with violence and abuse.

These ways of coping—whether society judges them as "good" or "bad"—help us get through. If you aren't a survivor of abuse or assault, they may not apply to you, or you may have other reasons for developing some of these traits.

WHAT ABUSE DID TO ME. If someone abused you as a child or an adult, note any ways that's influenced your ability to overcome (or challenge) denial, passivity, self-blame, or feelings of low self-worth. If you wish, think about ways the abuse influenced your actions in the experience you've been working with that you wrote down in Chapter 2.

Thinking about these experiences can be painful and can bring up memories and feelings of self-blame. Keep in mind that many of us share similar experiences (if not, we wouldn't need this book), and return to your self-care practices often.

Please avoid blaming yourself. Instead, aspire to have compassion for the ways you may have been conditioned to not resist.

_____

_____

_____

_____

_____

_____

CODEPENDENCE

One super common coping mechanism is codependence. Codependence occurs in intimate relationships where one person enables the other's addiction. More broadly, codependence is an unhelpful focus on people pleasing. Caring for someone is good. It's when our identities are focused on this caring, and it's one-way, that it becomes unhealthy.

Generally, if we're codependent, we need someone else to need us. When we support someone else's dysfunctional or toxic behavior, it's usually a way to try to make things better for ourselves, but in fact, codependence works against us.

One way it works against us is that it keeps us from knowing what we ourselves want and need, since our focus is on the other person's needs and how to meet them.

Codependence is tricky, because so many aspects of it align with the ways women and femmes are supposed to behave. It makes us vulnerable by:

- Discouraging self-care and self-protection
- Encouraging reacting to others rather than being aware of our own needs and desires and being able to say them
- Making us afraid of hurting someone's feelings or of being wrong
- Promoting self-blame and making excuses for another's behavior.

If codependence is part of your life—past or present—it'll affect your ability to protect and speak up for yourself.

MAKE IT PERSONAL. Do any of these describe you? Check the ones you relate to:

- ☐ I often put other people and their needs first.
- ☐ I often feel responsible for other people's feelings.
- ☐ I try to fix, change, or rescue others.
- ☐ My good feelings about who I am come from others liking or approving of me.
- ☐ I'm more aware of how others feel or what they want than I am of how I feel or what I want.

☐ It's hard for me to ask for what I want and need.

☐ My fear of others' anger or rejection determines what I say and do.

☐ I make excuses for others' weaknesses and have very high expectations of myself.

☐ I'm afraid of hurting others' feelings, of being wrong, or of their disapproval.

☐ I often blame myself and make excuses for others' behavior.

It's complicated: Some codependent behaviors can be wise survival measures if you're being abused. And some codependence is a dynamic of abuse as abusers try to make their partners responsible for the abuser's feelings and behaviors.

Let's pause for some breathing here. These exercises can be challenging. Please take a moment and get grounded in the present moment as much as you can.

Lauren's Story
My depressed mother

I was always trying to make my depressed mother happier. I did that mostly by trying hard not to have feelings or needs (or at least not to let them show). I believed that if she were happier, she'd love me. I wanted her to do something as simple as look at me and smile. But I wasn't in charge of my mother's happiness! I've spent most of my adult life trying to unlearn my belief that I have to make the people around me happy so they'll be able to love me.

WHOSE NEEDS FIRST? Look at your story from Chapter 2. Did any of the dynamics in the checklist affect your ability to avoid or respond to the situation? Did you put the other person's needs before your own?

_____

_____

This is a lot. You might feel discouraged looking at all that we're up against. But recognizing these societal dynamics and how they affect us can help us break free of them.

TL;DR

- Society blames victim-survivors for the harm done to us, making it harder for us to stand up for and protect ourselves.

- We face barriers to protecting ourselves: denial, passivity, self-blame, and feelings of low self-worth.

- Society's rigid and limited gender roles teach many of us to be quiet and passive—and punish us for stepping outside the lines.

- Barriers to protecting ourselves also come from oppression and from family dysfunction.

- When we take all that in, it can show up as self-blame and self-hate that make advocating for ourselves more difficult.

- Recognizing all these forces can help us break free from them.

THE HEART OF THE MATTER. *What's the best or most important thing you'll remember from this chapter? What's your favorite way to sum it up? Draw, doodle, tell a friend, record it on your phone—anything that works for you.*

SELF-CARE BREAK. *Take a deep breath. What self-care will you do now that you've finished this chapter? It can be a small thing (like a few seconds of stretching) or something bigger (like a day off). For more ideas, check in with the plan you made on page xix or the ideas we list on page 10.*

YOU DESERVE IT! *Pushing back against society's rules isn't easy. It calls for a great deal of courage and self-compassion. Recognize that and be good to yourself.*

Chapter 5

FIRST, YOU HAVE TO BELIEVE

You're Worth Defending

GROUNDING & CENTERING: Five-finger breathing. Put the index finger of one hand on the outside (the pinky side) of your other hand near your wrist. Move your index finger up the outside of the pinky on your other hand, and as you do so, slowly breathe in. Move up and down each finger, breathing in as you go up a finger and out as you go down. When you finish your thumb, go back across your hand in reverse. This exercise can be extra powerful because it combines breathing with the tactile experience of feeling your finger on your hand.

As we've seen, gender programming can lead us to believe we're not worthy or not valuable enough to protect or to speak up for. In this chapter, we hope to convince you that you're worth defending, that you're trustworthy when it comes to your feelings and your life, and that you have a right to be safe.

YOU ARE
ENOUGH.

PART 1

You Are Worth Defending

Our lives are precious. We deserve to be safe. We are worth defending. *You* are worth defending.

So many of us were told, even by our caregivers, that we were worthless, burdensome, not smart, incompetent, and so on. We were told we were liars, that our feelings didn't matter, that we were "too much," melodramatic—or simply wrong.

Here's the truth: all humans are valuable—you included.

I MATTER TOO. Think about someone in your life you care about. Think of at least three things you value about them.

Then imagine someone treating the person you care about disrespectfully or harming them in another way. Think of the reason(s) you believe your person should be safe and treated well.

Now turn that focus to yourself. Write at least three things you value about yourself. Don't make the entire list about how good you are to other people; while things like being a loyal or generous friend or a good listener can be on the list, make sure you also have plenty of things that aren't about what you do for others.

Then write the reason(s) you deserve to be safe and treated with respect.

_____

_____

_____

_____

_____

Now take a deep breath (or several), and allow your right to safety and respect to wash over you.

SEARCHING ALL DIRECTIONS WITH ONE'S AWARENESS, ONE FINDS NO ONE DEARER THAN ONESELF.

—The Buddha

Many of us find more compassion for ourselves when we connect with our younger self or our inner child who needs care and protection. For example, Nadia's more likely to stop and take a break when she pictures a part of herself that needs caretaking (like a child who's hungry) than when she relates to herself as an adult who can keep pushing without rest.

WHAT DO I NEED? Is there anything your inner child needs right now? Reassuring words, encouragement, reminders to practice self-care? If so, write it in a notebook (or doodle, draw, or tell a friend about it). You can include things your inner child needs at other times too.

Learning to value ourselves unconditionally is a first step to change. This means that we neither criticize ourselves for the time it takes to make changes nor blame ourselves for falling back into old thinking or behaviors; after all, we've had years of practice in those patterns and lots of reinforcement from family, friends, and society to stay there.

To change, we start with noticing our areas of difficulty. Then we can reward ourselves for our successes, however small, and above all, we can be patient with ourselves and with the process.

FAN THE FLAMES 2. "Energy follows attention" is an observation based on the ancient Chinese saying "Qi follows Yi"—what we focus on is what grows. We encourage you to focus on efforts you've made, however small, instead of on any regrets you have.

Think of times in your life when you've advocated for yourself. They don't have to be major, like breaking up with someone who was abusing you or fighting off a rape attempt, though they can be.

They can be smaller (small things are still hard!), like sending a dish back at a restaurant, telling your partner you need them to pitch in more with the kids or the housework, asking a roommate to remember to lock the door, asking for a raise, contacting the cellphone carrier about your bill, blocking someone who demands too much of you, not responding to work emails after hours, or telling a parent to stop commenting on your choice of partner.

In the space below or in a separate journal, write down some times you've set a boundary or asked for what you wanted.

_____

_____

_____

_____

_____

PART 2

You Are Trustworthy

You deserve kindness, care, safety. Everything you wish for others, you deserve too.

Because many of us weren't celebrated for who we are, we doubt our thoughts, feelings, and perceptions. Survivors of harassment, abuse, or assault also tend to doubt ourselves because people may not have believed us if we shared what was done to us, or they said it was our fault or it wasn't a big deal.

You deserve to be listened to by the people in your life and, most importantly, by yourself.

Trusting yourself means taking action to protect yourself and honoring your need to be careful, even if you're not sure if you're about to be harassed or assaulted, and even if you're not sure that what's happening—or what happened—is abuse.

Sometimes if we can test our perceptions or check them with others, it's wise to do so. But if you tend to believe that everyone knows what's going on better than you do—and you look to others to tell you what you "should" feel—it's time to explore honoring yourself.

THE ROOTS OF SELF-DOUBT. Where do you think you got your self-doubt from? (Some possibilities: gender-role training, past abuse, messages from specific people—like those who raised you—or others' reactions based on racism, sexism, or some other form of oppression.) Write or draw your thoughts below or in a journal.

INTUITION

One consequence of not valuing ourselves is that many of us aren't in touch with our intuition, or gut feeling, which exists to protect us. Part of learning to trust yourself is connecting with and listening to your intuition.

Do you know that feeling you have when you sense that something's wrong but you're not sure what? That's your intuition. It's important to be in touch with it, because your unconscious mind, which takes in information super quickly through all five senses, often knows when something or someone's a problem before your thinking brain does.

We get the result of all that information—a feeling—without knowing why. Later, we may be able to reconstruct some of the signals that led to our intuitive response.

Even if you're in touch with your intuition, it can be difficult to trust it. The dominant cultures in the U.S. for the most part value only the logical and rational. What's usually called "women's intuition" doesn't get the respect it deserves.

Acting on your intuition requires trusting yourself and believing in your right to act even if there's a chance you could be wrong about what's going on. You may never find out what the other person's intentions were. But if you wait for "proof" that there's a problem, things may have gotten worse.

Anh's Story
Listen to yourself

After agreeing to go out to dinner with Stephan, a coworker with whom she had enjoyed many good conversations, Anh had a feeling she shouldn't be alone with him. She asked another coworker to be with her when she canceled the date. Stephan got very angry, screamed at them both, and said he even cleaned his apartment and bought beer to get ready for the evening. Anh was glad she listened to her intuition because he'd had plans for a different kind of date than what she'd agreed to.

Is intuition always present? Nope! There's nothing wrong with you if you didn't have an intuitive warning about an assault—that's pretty common.

It can be easy to confuse intuition and worry. One difference is that, usually, intuition comes to us as a physical feeling, while we worry in our heads.

If you frequently have feelings that something's wrong, there are some other possibilities. One is that you may be experiencing anxiety, for although harassment and assault are frequent, they're generally not constant. Second, you may be experiencing ongoing abuse, or you may be responding to past trauma. If ongoing abuse or past trauma is at play, please see page 245 for resources that can help you.

HELLO, SPIDEY. To find out how your intuition talks to you, ask a trusted friend to be at least six feet away and then move slowly toward you. When you feel like they're close enough without being *too* close, tell them to stop. Stand there for a few seconds noting how the distance feels.

Then ask your friend to get one foot closer—they should now be *too* close. Stay with it for a few seconds and notice where in your body the "NOT OKAY!" feeling is. Then ask your friend to step away. Be sure to breathe and shake it out when you're done (it's uncomfortable!).

That "NOT OKAY!" feeling can show up anywhere in your body and with a zillion possible sensations. Lauren usually feels it as a tightness in her chest and a bit of a feeling that she can't breathe. Sometimes she feels a clutching in her stomach and diaphragm or solar plexus. Many people feel a need to back up or feel their heart beat faster, their hands tighten into fists, their palms sweat, their jaw clench, or even, literally, the hair on the back of their neck stand up.

You can do this exercise over and over to get familiar with how your body talks to you. Then the important thing is to pay attention when you have that feeling and to *take action*. You don't have to understand *why*, just listen to yourself.

In *The Gift of Fear*, Gavin de Becker highlights the fact that humans are the only animals who talk ourselves out of our self-protective instincts, putting ourselves at greater risk.

> *Can you imagine an animal reacting to the gift of fear the way some people do, with annoyance and disdain instead of attention? No animal in the wild, suddenly overcome with fear, would spend any of its mental energy thinking, "It's probably nothing." Yet we chide ourselves for even momentarily giving validity to the feeling that someone is behind us on a seemingly empty street or that someone's unusual behavior might be sinister. Instead of being grateful to have a powerful internal resource, grateful for the self-care, instead of entertaining the possibility that our minds might actually be working for us and not just playing tricks on us, we rush to ridicule the impulse. . . . The mental energy we use searching for the innocent explanation to everything could more constructively be applied to evaluating the environment for important information.*

There's nothing wrong with *you*. The fault lies with the social forces that separated you from your self-protective instincts.

I DO BELIEVE. With a friend standing close or on your own, summon your Spidey Sense, the feeling that something's wrong. Imagine a stressful or challenging situation (like someone standing too close or touching you when you don't want them to). Notice what's happening in your body. Then think about what you could say or do to take action—set a limit, leave, tell the other person to back up, or anything that works for you (we'll have more on what to say in Chapter 9).

Do any barriers to speaking up appear? "I'm not sure if they mean anything by it," "Maybe I'm being oversensitive," "I want them to like me," or anything else? Now's the time to get used to ignoring that pushback so you can take action to keep yourself safe not just physically but emotionally, mentally, spiritually, and psychically. Does your brain tell you not to trust or value yourself? If it does, turn to the barrier and talk to it. Some things you can say to it are:

- "Please leave."
- "Do you have anything important to tell me? If not, buh-bye!"
- "You're not helping me."
- "I hear you and I choose not to listen to you."

CELEBRATING MY INTUITION. Affirmations are positive statements in the present tense that offer emotional support or encouragement. (We'll talk more about affirmations in Chapter 6.) Below are two examples of situations where you might use affirmations to bolster your right to listen to your intuition and to set a limit. In the first drawing, the seated person is talking themselves out of their feelings. In the second drawing, write in the dialogue bubbles what you could say to yourself to affirm your intuition.

1. You're at a coffee shop and someone starts making conversation with you. You just want to read.

2. You're in a supermarket parking lot when someone from your neighborhood comes up to you. His arm's in a sling, and he wants you to help him get to his car. Again, in the second drawing, write in the dialogue bubbles what you could say to yourself to affirm your intuition and your right not to do what someone's asking.

This example shows how your intuition might work. It probably wondered why he wasn't using a cart. Why he didn't get help from someone in the store. Why he parked so far from the door. Even without your conscious brain noticing these facts, your intuition's protecting you by taking them in. (This is similar to the ploys serial killer Ted Bundy used.)

FAN THE FLAMES 3. To build your trust in the intuitive part of your brain, it's helpful to recognize when it's served you well. Think of a time when you made a decision or took an action based on a sense or feeling rather than on a "rational" thought, then write what happened. How did your intuition speak to you? What do you think made you notice it? Do you know how you decided what to do?

This doesn't have to do only with safety. Maybe you decided what to study, where to live, or whether to take a job. Perhaps you felt a pull to go back to a place you'd been, only to discover you'd left something there. Or maybe your intuition told you something was okay, even though on the surface it seemed risky. If you can't think of anything, you might ask friends about their experiences and use an example from one of them.

_____

_____

_____

_____

_____

_____

_____

_____

_____

_____

_____

Especially If You're White

Spidey Sense and racism

U.S. society and culture constantly broadcast messages that Black and Brown men are dangerous and threatening. Because of that, it can sometimes be hard to tell the difference between racism-fueled anxiety and intuition.

If you feel anxious, uncomfortable, even threatened, you might be unsure if the feeling is your intuition speaking or if it's the racism that everyone—especially White people—in this country learns growing up.

The fact is, if you're attacked, it's most likely to be by someone of your own race. (Two notes: First, this isn't true if you're Indigenous; you're more likely to be attacked by a White person. And second, this is, of course, more complex for multiracial people.)

To get some clarity about whether the fear you feel is based in reality, ask yourself whether you're looking at the person's *behavior* or their *identity*. To assess risk, we want to look at behavior.

Are they asking questions that are too personal? Touching you when you don't want to be touched? Threatening or coercing you? Not respecting other boundaries? Think of some other things that would be red flags to you. If they're doing one of these, you're assessing danger based on behavior.

If you're not Black or Brown and often feel fear or anxiety when you're around Black or Brown men, but there's no behavior you can point to that's causing it, that's probably racist programming.

A centuries-long history of White women weaponizing White womanhood has caused violence and death to Black people of all genders, especially men and boys. The terrorist gang murder of fourteen-year-old Emmett Till after Carolyn Bryant, a White woman, falsely accused him of flirting with her is an infamous example. More recently, Amy Cooper, angry that a Black man (Christian Cooper, no relation) reminded her that her dog needed to be leashed in the park, called the police and told them, "An African American man is threatening my life." Violence like this plays out every day.

Unless White and other non-Black people are consciously engaged in unlearning racism, we're liable to cause racist harm ourselves.

Of course, attackers can have any identity. And sometimes intuition does send out alerts even when there's no problematic behavior. But much of the time, looking at behavior (as opposed to identity) can be a useful tool in evaluating danger.

PART 3

You Have Rights, and Knowing Them Gives You Power

As humans, we have the right to be safe and to be treated well. In a world that's unsafe for women, BIPOC, and LGBTQIA+ people, among others, we have the right to do whatever we need to do in order to be as safe as we can. It might be difficult for you to embrace this right.

Take a minute to center and ground yourself using one of the exercises from the start of a chapter. Then think about your own rights having to do with safety, empowerment, and self-defense. (We have other rights too, like the right to clean water and free speech, but that's not what we're talking about here.)

A list of rights can serve as a touchstone as you live your life. They may be nearly universal ("I have the right to be safe") or very particular to you ("I have the right to wear zebra-striped green eyeshadow without my partner criticizing me for it").

Here are some rights our students have written for themselves.

I Have a Right To:

- Ask for what I want
- Be in public spaces, including online, without harassment
- Be treated with respect at home, work, school, in public, and everywhere
- Be safe in my home
- Be spoken to calmly, without yelling
- Be touched only with consent
- Change my mind
- Come and go as I please without being monitored
- Defend myself, including fighting back if attacked
- Define my own comfort zone
- Feel however I feel without my feelings being minimized or ignored
- Feel like my body is my own

- Have my boundaries respected
- Have my feelings, including anger
- Have sex only when I want to
- Insist on safer sex and/or on birth control use
- Make mistakes
- Make my own decisions
- Put myself first
- Refuse sex with someone I've been sexual with before, or say "no" to sex acts even if I've done them before
- Say "no" once and be heard
- Set limits with emotionally draining friends
- Speak my mind
- Take care of myself, not just others
- Take up space in the world
- Walk around any time of the day and not be attacked
- Wear what I want
- Work without being harassed.

The flip side of rights is responsibilities. Others deserve these rights just as we do. It's our responsibility to communicate in a positive and nonviolent way, to treat others with respect, and to listen to the boundaries they set. (That doesn't mean that if we fail to do one or more of these things and someone harms us that it's our fault. It's not.)

MY RIGHTS. Prioritize your well-being. Choose some of the rights from the list that resonate with you. Using the space on the following page, a notebook, or a phone or computer, make a list of your rights, adding any others you want. Rights can be big or small, general or incredibly specific. Write as many as you can think of.

Having your rights—or just a few of them—somewhere you can easily see them can be super useful. Put them on the refrigerator or the bathroom mirror. Take a photo of your list (or write it in your phone) and carry it with you. Your list can help you when you feel your rights are being disrespected, when you're uncomfortable, or when you're not sure what to do.

MY RIGHTS

Taking up more space, setting boundaries, asking for what you want: The people in your life probably won't all celebrate these changes, and they may even push back hard. But the cost of not doing them—of living small and putting ourselves last—is too high for most of us.

BUT EVENTUALLY, I JUST GOT TIRED OF ALWAYS WORRYING ABOUT WHAT EVERYONE ELSE THOUGHT OF ME. SO I DECIDED NOT TO LISTEN.

—Michelle Obama

PATRIARCHY CHICKEN. Pay attention to where you take up space—literal space. If you're not a cis man, practice not yielding to men in public spaces like the sidewalk or a fast-food restaurant. (If you're White, only do this with White men, so you don't perpetuate racism.) Check out what happens when you don't move out of the way. How do you feel when you don't move? Do you have a right to space on the sidewalk or in the hallway? (Trust your intuition if this feels risky at any given moment.)

Anna's Story

Collision in the grocery store

Anna was at the store with her six-year-old daughter. They were heading to the door with their cart and a White man was heading straight for them. He wouldn't move. It was a pretty small store, and Anna had already noticed how most women moved over when they saw her and her daughter coming. She decided she wasn't moving. Unfortunately, he didn't move either! Anna tried to move at the last minute, but it was too late. He walked straight into their cart. He did apologize, though. As Anna said, "I guess there's hope for him!"

WHAT I SAID WAS... You can also take up space with your voice. With family, at the workplace, in faith groups, and among friends or neighbors: All of these can be places where men talk over or interrupt us. They may also act as if we never said what we said, parroting our ideas and opinions like they're saying them for the first time.

List some phrases you can say in that situation and use them as needed. Here are a few to get started and a place to add your own:

Reclaiming My Time
(Thanks, Representative Maxine Waters!)

What I said was . . .	
Please let me finish.	
As I said earlier . . .	
I was speaking.	
I just said that.	

AMPLIFY AND BOOST. Learn from what the women in the Obama administration did when they couldn't get a word in or when their contributions were ignored. As Juliet Eilperin reported in *The Washington*

Post, they "adopted a strategy they called 'amplification': When a woman made a key point, other women would repeat it, giving credit to its author. This forced the men in the room to recognize the contribution—and denied them the chance to claim the idea as their own."

Consider making a commitment with the women, LGBTQIA+ people, BIPOC men, and other marginalized people at your workplace or school that when they're interrupted or talked over, or when their ideas are ignored, you'll repeat what they said, giving credit to the originator. You can also ask allies to do the same.

Write the names of those you'll ask to start doing this practice with you.

_____

_____

_____

_____

_____

_____

TL;DR

- If society and those who raised you told you that you're less than amazing, powerful, and valuable, they were wrong!

- You can learn to trust yourself: your intuition, your judgment, your knowledge of what you need to be safe.

- While society bombards all of us, regardless of race, with messages that Black and Brown people are threatening and dangerous, you can unlearn that and discern where the real risks lie.

- You have rights. Claiming and embracing them will help you step into your power.

THE HEART OF THE MATTER. *What's your main takeaway from this chapter? Did something resonate with you—an insight, a new understanding or perspective? Write it down, text it to a friend, or draw it.*

SELF-CARE BREAK. *Take a deep breath. What self-care will you do now that you've finished this chapter? It can be a small thing (like a few seconds of stretching) or something bigger (like a day off). For more ideas, check in with the plan you made on page xix or the ideas we list on page 10.*

YOU GOT THIS! *You're challenging what you know about yourself and the world. Shaking things up like that can destabilize you—and it can strengthen you as you embrace a more authentic you.*

Chapter 6

CLAIM YOUR POWER

GROUNDING & CENTERING: There's something about a sound. Sing, yell, hum, chant. Growl. If being loud isn't an option, say encouraging or inspiring words to yourself quietly or in your head. Say affirmations or assertive statements. Making sounds can help you be present to yourself, and it gets your breath going.

To defend ourselves, we must believe it's okay to take care of ourselves, sometimes putting our needs and feelings before those of others. We have to become willing to hurt someone else's feelings, or even their body, to protect ourselves. This may go against how we were taught to focus on nurturing and caring for others.

To become someone who can do this, many of us will need to get in touch with our feelings, needs, and wants; tame our inner critics; and start to celebrate our successes—even the little ones. In this chapter, you'll learn to do all that.

"YOU'RE BRAVER THAN YOU BELIEVE, STRONGER THAN YOU SEEM, AND SMARTER THAN YOU THINK."

—Christopher Robin in *Pooh's Grand Adventure: The Search for Christopher Robin*

PART 1

Tune Back In: Get in Touch with Your Feelings, Needs, and Wants

Because we learn to accommodate and prioritize others, we often decide our limits based on what we can tolerate as opposed to what we really need or want. "Can I put up with—or get through—this?" is a question that stomps all over our own selves.

And just to make all that more problematic, we probably also believe that we can't speak up unless we're *sure* the other person plans to harm us.

In fact, it doesn't matter what the other person intends—if they "mean anything by it." What matters is how it's affecting you. You have a right to your feelings, needs, and wants. In focusing on those, you won't get waylaid trying to figure out someone else's intentions.

To change that disconnection—and that focus on what we can bear—we'll start with being able to get in touch with a feeling in your body and then put a name to it. The next step is taking the feeling and translating it into what you want to happen. Then you'll be able to set a boundary or ask for what you want.

I'M GONNA HAVE FEELINGS ABOUT THIS... Look at the feelings wheel pictured here. Then look at the list of situations on page 104. Pick a few situations and after each one, write the words that express what you're likely to feel in that situation. Feel free to make up your own words and add your own feelings.

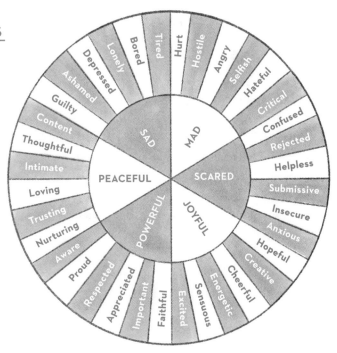

- Someone cuts you off in traffic or drives too close to you.

  _____

- Someone at your job or school stands too close when they talk to you.

  _____

- You get a raise.

  _____

- Someone harasses you on the street and when you frown at them, they say, "It's a compliment."

  _____

- You wake up in the morning and realize it's your day off.

  _____

- You're arguing with a friend and they turn to leave.

  _____

- You're waiting to hear if you got the job/gig/part.

  _____

- A family member criticizes your appearance.

  _____

- Someone you're dating tells you that you're "pretty for a . . . [insert a marginalized identity here]."

  _____

- You hear that you got the job/gig/part.

  _____

- Someone you're not into tells you they love you.

  _____

- You're at a club or party and someone you don't know puts their hands on you.

  _____

- You're waiting to hear about test results.

  _____

- You hear that you didn't get the job/gig/part.

  _____

- A romantic partner puts you down in front of friends.

  _____

- Someone you love has a big success.

  _____

- Your crush doesn't text you back for four hours.

  _____

- You tell a friend/partner that something they do is hard for you and ask them to stop doing it. They keep doing it.

  _____

- You hear about a natural disaster.

  _____

- Your ex keeps showing up wherever you are.

  _____

- You're a woman, and a man at work or school says to you, "You should smile more."

  _____

- You get an award at work or a great report card.

  _____

- A friend spreads rumors about you.

  _____

- A family member keeps using your deadname.

  _____

  _____

A **deadname** is the name a trans or non-binary person was given at birth and no longer uses. Also a verb, as in "Please stop dead-naming me."

- Someone you love says they love you.

  _____

- Someone in your friend circle tells a "joke" about girls/women/LGBTQIA+ people/ people of color/fat people/disabled people/etc.

  _____

- You come into your home, and your bag of groceries breaks and everything spills everywhere.

  _____

- A coworker or classmate "accidentally" touches your butt.

  _____

MY FEELINGS RAINBOW 1. In the center of the rainbow are our feelings, needs, and wants. Around them are messages that keep us from being in touch with those feelings, like "Don't be rude," "Don't hurt anyone's feelings," or "It's not a big deal."

Choose a story from Chapter 2. What do you think the person who was being targeted felt, needed, and wanted? Write that in the center of the rainbow below.

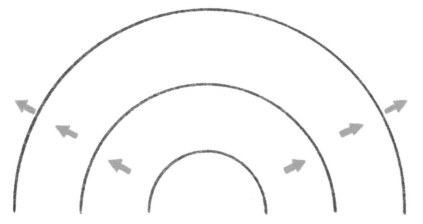

Messages that kept the person in the story from identifying their feelings, needs, and wants

In the rainbow arches, write any messages that might've gotten in the way of the person being targeted saying—or acting on—what they felt, needed, or wanted.

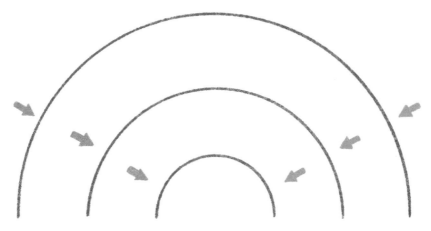

Messages that help the person in the story identify their feelings, needs, and wants

Now, in this rainbow, write some encouragement for the person who was being targeted. What might you say to help them honor their feelings, needs, and wants? (You can get ideas from "I Have a Right To" in Chapter 5.)

MY FEELINGS RAINBOW 2. Look at your own story from Chapter 2 or at another time when you struggled to say what you felt, needed, or wanted. In the center of the rainbow, write what you felt, needed, and wanted in that situation.

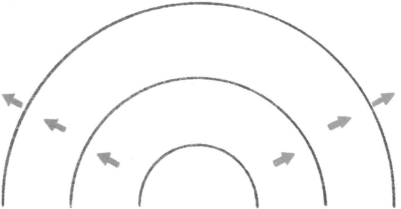

Messages that kept you from identifying your feelings, needs, and wants

In the arches of the rainbow, write any messages that made it difficult for you to identify, say, or act on these feelings, needs, and wants, such as, "You'll embarrass them if you say anything," "Don't hurt their feelings," or "You're so sensitive."

In the last rainbow, write some encouragement for future you. Practice honoring your own feelings, needs, and wants by creating affirmations, rights, or reminders that can help you identify and say all three of them.

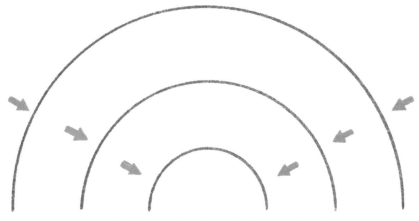

Messages that help you identify your feelings, needs, and wants

Learning to set limits, advocate for yourself, and be an active resister means being able to move past the conditioning that makes those things hard. Having an inner coach can help you get there.

Like a BFF who's always in your corner, a coach can help you honor what you think, see, hear, and feel—and act based on those things. If you come from a lineage or culture where ancestors show up for you, an ancestor can be helpful here. No matter who you choose, they can support you when you're not feeling the energy to do it for yourself. Your coach might, for example, remind you of your rights, cheer you on, or affirm your value. You can call on them when you feel unsure or need a boost.

Your coach can also give you care, attention, and comfort during difficult times, and they can help you heal afterward.

FEEL, NEED, WANT—AND CONSENT. Thinking about greetings is one way to explore what you feel, need, and want, and what kinds of touch work for you. When you see someone you feel close to, what's your favorite way to greet them? A wave, a fist bump, a handshake, a short—or long—hug? Does the greeting change based on context or on how you're feeling that day? Does it change depending on the person? How do you let people know which greeting you prefer? If someone moves to give you a higher-contact greeting than the one you prefer, how do you communicate what's okay with you and what's not? If someone wants less contact than you do, how do you negotiate that and respect their consent needs? Write your answers here.

_____

_____

_____

_____

_____

_____

TEAM ME. Envision your coach. Do they have a name? What do they look like? They don't have to be someone you know; they can be an animal, an energy source, a deity, a celebrity, or anything else that works for you. What's their energy like? How do you feel when you're around them? Write, draw, or record what you know about your coach. You can check in with them as you work with *Get Empowered*.

CHANGE THE NARRATIVE. One thing your coach can do is help you to cut through the messages that cause you to neglect—or reject—your feelings, needs, and wants. Instead, your coach will help you honor them. Write or draw some encouraging things this coach might say to you. (Here are a few examples to get you started.) Then say them to yourself out loud or silently.

ME	MY COACH
They probably don't like me. If I say something, they'll think I'm a pain in the ass (or I'm needy).	If they only like you when you silence parts of yourself, they don't like the real you. Being liked isn't necessarily the most important thing.
I'm not sure what I want, and they seem certain. I'll just do what they want. No big deal.	Your feelings and needs are as important as anyone else's. If you don't speak up for yourself, who will?
What if I'm wrong? What if they don't mean anything by it?	Your safety is more important than someone else's comfort.

WHEN YOU'RE NOT USED TO BEING CONFIDENT, CONFIDENCE FEELS LIKE ARROGANCE. WHEN YOU'RE USED TO BEING PASSIVE, ASSERTIVENESS FEELS LIKE AGGRESSION. WHEN YOU'RE NOT USED TO GETTING YOUR NEEDS MET, PRIORITIZING YOURSELF FEELS SELFISH. YOUR COMFORT ZONE IS NOT A GOOD BENCHMARK.

—*Dr. Vassilia Binensztok*

PART 2

Tame the Inner Critic

Negative self-talk comes from many places. The more we understand its source, the better we're able to see a realistic balance of the positive, negative, and neutral.

Throughout the ages, humans who were more aware of—and influenced by—the negative than the positive were more likely to survive. This hardwired tendency to imagine the worst helped the species stay alive when tigers could have eaten us and when we faced other threats to survival.

This doesn't mean we're destined to sink into negativity. Just being aware of how negativity bias is meant to help us is a first step in overcoming it.

Compounding negativity bias is our programming to prioritize others; it's one reason so many of us have powerful inner critics. We think we need to be perfect to be safe and lovable. When we're not perfect (it's impossible . . . no one is), our inner critic lets us know, and know hard.

We talk to ourselves the way we'd never talk to anyone else, saying things like "I'll never be any good at this," "I can't believe I did this again," "I hate myself," "I'm stupid," or "Nobody will ever like me."

So we focus on the ways we think we're "not good enough." Negative self-talk can be so constant that it seems normal, and we don't realize how much hate and negativity we spew at ourselves. It can be made up of things other people have said to us, especially things we heard when we were young. If we were treated as fragile, needy, "too much," or incompetent, we're likely to fulfill those expectations (unless we take those messages as a challenge or do a lot of work to change that). If we were treated as capable and expected to be able to do things, it's more likely we'll be able to.

Negative self-talk is also a function of the interwoven oppressive systems we live in: patriarchy, White supremacy, capitalism, and others. We absorb these systems' values and beliefs, but we can forget that they come from those oppressive systems and instead come to see them as our own. But "lazy," "needy," "unproductive," and "ugly" are straight-up examples of social and cultural stereotypes about those who aren't cis, White, able-bodied, straight men.

Negative self-talk damages our minds, our hearts, our spirits, our relationships, and our bodies (in the form of stress). It limits our dreams and our potential. It makes our lives way harder than they need to be.

We can't think or commit our way out of negative self-talk. Arguing with an inner critic doesn't change its ways. We can't force our inner critics to leave us alone. But with more awareness of those voices and thoughts, and through practice to relate to them differently, we can learn to treat ourselves better.

MY INNER CRITIC IN THE SPOTLIGHT. Pick a time—say, an hour every morning for a week or one full day. In that time, focus on noticing when you speak to yourself in a way you wouldn't speak to someone you cared about. Each time you notice it, take a conscious breath.

CHANGE MY INNER MONOLOGUE. Now that you're noticing when your inner critic is doing its thing, let's work on taking some of the power out of it. One technique is to simply name what's happening: "My inner critic is saying mean things to me." "I'm being harsh to myself right now." This helps you remove the shame and get more realistic about what's happening, rather than spinning off into a probably familiar rut.

After you've done this for a week, a month, or a year, try reshaping what your inner critic is saying into something objective and true. Below are some examples, and space to add your own.

IF YOU HEAR...	TRANSLATE IT INTO...
I can't do this.	I'm not feeling ready or able to do this.
	This task feels too hard.
	I need more practice.
	This is challenging.

IF YOU HEAR...	TRANSLATE IT INTO...
I should be able to handle this.	I'm putting "shoulds" on myself. I'm doing the best I can. I'm doing a lot.
I can't believe I said that—I'm such an asshole.	I regret what I said.
I'm stupid/a failure/an idiot. I'm a coward.	I'm calling myself names and using put-downs. I failed at this one thing.
I can't see that person/do that thing until I lose weight.	I'm limiting my options based on my size.
I have nothing to say or contribute. No one wants to hear me anyway. My thoughts on this aren't important. Everyone else is smarter/wiser/better informed than I am.	I believe my contributions aren't valuable.
I'm a fake. I'm going to be found out.	I'm doubting my expertise and worth, and I'm afraid to be vulnerable. I'm feeling like an imposter.
If only I didn't waste time, I'd have achieved all my goals. I don't work hard enough. I'm such a slacker.	I'm criticizing my productivity and judging how I spend my time.
Last time I saw them I was happier/younger/fitter/thinner/cuter. They'll think I'm stupid/ugly/depressing/old now. I should just stay home.	I'm imagining what others think of me. I don't really know what they think or how they feel.

IF YOU HEAR...	TRANSLATE IT INTO...
I'll never be as good as so-and-so at that.	I'm comparing myself with someone else.
I'm a terrible parent. No one else's kids would ever behave like that.	I'm judging my parenting.
I can't believe I screwed that up.	I made a mistake, and I'm being hard on myself about it.
If I can do it, it must not be very difficult or special or worthwhile. Anyone could do it.	I'm devaluing my strengths and skills.
No one likes me. I don't have any friends.	I'm feeling lonely. I crave connection.

Remember that while you may have said or done something you regret, it's not who you are. Once you take who you are out of the equation, "I'm so stupid" becomes "I did a stupid thing" or "I'm feeling stupid"—a small but powerful change.

A LITTLE COMPASSION. No one's perfect. Everyone makes mistakes. You're doing the best you can.

Chances are you've heard these clichés and thought they didn't really apply to you. But if someone you loved was talking about themselves the way you talk about yourself, you'd definitely be kind to them.

You deserve kindness too. Below, write some kind and nurturing phrases you can say to yourself, such as:

- I appreciate you.
- You're doing the best you can.
- This sounds really hard.
- It's okay to be imperfect.
- You're allowed to rest.
-
-
-
-

Or take a page from Buddhism and say some self-compassion phrases to yourself. Here are some ideas; you can use these or create your own.

- May I be kind and gentle with myself.
- May I trust that I'm doing my best.
- May I cultivate patience with myself.
- May I forgive myself.
- May I treat myself with kindness.
- May I trust that I am enough.
- May I love myself as I am.
-
-
-
-

GREET THE TROLL. Have a chat with your inner critic. Be curious and ask it questions. "What are the reasons you're saying I'll never be good enough?" "Is there something important you want to tell me?"

In listening to the answers, you'll probably find that your inner critic's trying to be helpful or trying to protect you in some way. The inner critic kept us quiet, helping us stay safe or cared for in our families growing up.

But it's no longer helpful; it isn't keeping you safe anymore. Tell it, "Thank you for trying to help me," and let it know that you can handle the situation. You can do this over and over as you build a healthier, more loving relationship with yourself. If you like, write down what you want the inner critic to hear from you.

_____

_____

_____

_____

I'M NOT ALONE. Your inner critic and negative self-talk feed on secrecy and shame. Write down any awful, judgmental things you think about yourself. Include your thoughts about any time you made mistakes or decisions you feel guilt or regret about. (Remember, you have other choices besides literal writing. Do whatever works for you.)

Think of one person in your life you can share the truth with. Start by telling them the least awful thing you've got, and invite them to share theirs. Make clear before you start if you want a response or just someone to listen. Breathe, and thank yourself and them for taking this risk together.

Remember again that the things you're struggling with aren't your personal quirks or shortcomings. A summary of Ruchika Tulshyan and Jodi-Ann Burey's article about imposter syndrome in *Harvard Business Review* said it well:

> *"Imposter syndrome," or doubting your abilities and feeling like a fraud at work, is a diagnosis often given to women. But the fact that it's considered a diagnosis at all is problematic. The concept, whose development in the 1970s excluded the effects of systemic racism, classism, xenophobia, and other biases, took a fairly universal feeling of discomfort, second-guessing, and mild anxiety in the workplace and pathologized it, especially for women. The answer to overcoming imposter syndrome is not to fix individuals but to create an environment that fosters a number of different leadership styles and where diversity of racial, ethnic, and gender identities is viewed as just as professional as the current model.*

Realizing that it's not a personal problem but a systemic one, and that we're pretty much all in it together, can take the power out of negative self-talk. As one person shared with us:

> *It's strangely reassuring to know you're not the only one carrying the burden of self-criticism even after thousands of hours of therapy, meditation, inner and outer work. We really are, all of us, in the muck together. Maybe seeing this so clearly will help us get out from under the burden we're each carrying.*

PART 3

You Can Change Your Thinking

If you've been alive in the U.S. since the '80s, you probably know about affirmations. Silly as they may sound, they're powerful ways to change our thinking and our experience. While we're learning to speak up for ourselves, set boundaries, and protect ourselves, affirmations give us a way out of the hole our inner critic is digging for us and a foundation on which to start building those skills.

Affirmations counter negative self-talk and open the door for change. Just as you construct a building by first creating a drawing of it, so you create change by first creating a positive image or statement.

Affirmations speak to your unconscious. For them to be effective:

- Make them simple. Example: "I'm strong and capable."

- Make them positive. Example: "I'm a strong person" instead of "I'm not weak." (If you say, "I'm not weak," your brain picks up on "weak," just like how you can't help but think about elephants when someone tells you, "Don't think about elephants.")

- Make them present tense. Example: "I speak up when I'm uncomfortable" instead of "I will speak up when I'm uncomfortable."

Don't argue with negative self-talk, and don't go overboard showering yourself with praise. For example, if your self-talk says, "I suck at this," don't say, "You're amazing at this!" Instead, try giving yourself an instruction like "Time to pause for a deep breath."

Surround your affirmations with clear and detailed images. For example, imagine yourself as strong and capable. What are you like? How do you feel? What do you do as a strong and capable person? Add details, like colors that reflect strength and capability. How do you sit or stand when you're acting from your strength? Here are some affirmations to get you started.

- I believe in myself.
- I am enough.
- I honor what I feel.
- I speak up when others mistreat me.
- I trust my inner wisdom.
- I take care of myself.

Sometimes a full-on affirmation isn't possible. If that happens, affirm what you can. For example, if "I believe in myself" feels out of reach in the moment, try "I aspire to believe in myself" or "When I'm not fully believing in myself, I still pay attention to my needs."

Nadia's Story
Affirmations at work

I was planning to go to a conference and didn't feel good about it. I didn't even really want to go. I decided to try affirmations, so for a week or two before the conference, I repeated to myself, "I'm learning a lot and having a wonderful time." At one point during the event, I stopped and said to myself, "My good-ness. I *am* learning a lot and having a wonderful time!"

ON A POSITIVE NOTE. Write some affirmations for yourself. If images speak to you, draw or doodle them.

Repeat these affirmations to yourself often, especially just before going to sleep or when you wake up. Put them on your mirror, refrigerator, notebook, cellphone case, home screen, or dashboard—anywhere you'll see them often.

When you say an affirmation, your inner critic may argue with you. When that happens, revise your inner monologue (like in the chart on page 112) or ask the inner critic questions (like the exercise on page 116). Thank the inner critic for trying to help you, then switch back to your positive, present-tense affirmation.

You may find it difficult to believe affirmations work, and the "but . . ." may take over. Remember: It took a long time to learn the negative patterns, and it will take a while to learn new ones. The important thing is to practice and be patient with yourself.

PART 4

Find Your Successes

Another way negativity bias manifests is that we may do 1,572,964 things "right" (things we accomplished, that were satisfying, that we feel good about, that align with who we are or aspire to be), but if there's *one* thing we wish we'd done differently or "better," we'll obsess about that. Admit it: we'll probably beat ourselves up about it.

And so we're internally bombarded with ways we're not good enough, which gets in the way of change.

When it comes to standing up for ourselves, one way this shows up is in how we tell our stories. Because Nadia and Lauren are empowerment self-defense teachers, students often share with us and their classmates examples of times someone's crossed their boundaries. The stories usually sound like a version of this:

> *I was out of town for work, and a local colleague was giving me a ride to my hotel. They put their hand on my thigh and started rubbing my leg. I was totally stunned and afraid they'd go for my crotch or drive us to a deserted area. I felt extra trapped because my suitcase was in the trunk of the car. I told them I was uncomfortable and asked them to stop several*

times, but they didn't. I thought of opening the door and jumping out. I got louder and louder until I was yelling. Finally I told them that if they didn't stop touching me and drive me straight to the hotel, I'd tell their boss about what they were doing. They stopped. Afterward I called a hotline for support and I reported them to HR. What should I have done?

See how hard we are on ourselves? The first thing Lauren asks a student with an experience like that is: "Tell me what you did do." While they were sharing their story, Lauren heard the things the student did to protect themselves, but the student didn't.

If you focus only on what you didn't do, you're telling yourself a story that reinforces your belief in your own incompetence or your belief that you have no choices or power.

It's only when we recognize what we did do that we can claim our skills, our creativity, our instincts for self-preservation, and our competence. If we're always telling ourselves that we can't, we fail to recognize the times we *have* defended ourselves. If we honor the times we've advocated for ourselves, we can fan those flames!

The next step in transforming yourself into someone who can set boundaries and ask for what you want is to note when you do it or have done it in the past.

We all have, even if we feel like we haven't. It could be as small as asking for more ketchup or a different appointment time—or saying, "I can't talk now." It could be bigger, like saying "no" when someone asks to copy your homework or to touch your hair.

We don't define "success" as getting what you want from others. We have no control over other people's responses; the success comes from asking for what we want or in setting a boundary.

In this section, you'll have an opportunity to identify your strengths and build on your successes, however large or small they seem. In going through the exercises, you'll gain skills for keeping yourself safe and well—and changing unhelpful behavior.

You'll likely relate to some exercises more than others. As always, concentrate on those most useful to you.

Lauren's Story

Not a doormat

In empowerment self-defense classes, I give students homework asking them to think of a time they stood up for themselves, no matter how small.

Once a student came back the next week and said she had absolutely no examples—she'd never done it; she was a complete doormat. I said I was sure she had and that I'd help her brainstorm, and I'd check in with her every couple of classes and see if she'd thought of anything.

I was also thinking that between classes she might tell someone she couldn't give them a ride or something like that, and she'd have her success.

The following week she came back to class and said, "Oh, I have something. I forgot last week. I left an abusive husband."

!!!

This is the power of self-criticism—and of negativity bias—that we can forget something as monumental and life changing as leaving an abuser.

And when we do recognize something we've done well, we often devalue it, along the lines of: "If I can do it, it's not a big deal."

Nadia's Story

My brilliant mechanic

I had a friend who had an impressive aptitude for mechanical problem-solving. In particular, she was really good at fixing cars. At one point, she diagnosed a problem a mechanic's shop couldn't. In addition to diagnostics, she could often make repairs for her money-strapped friends using creative means.

But she devalued what she could do. She didn't realize how extraordinary her abilities were. Because of this thinking, she didn't give herself credit for her skills—and she got impatient with people who weren't able to do what she did.

Once you start noticing what you've done to set limits, ask for what you want, and protect your mind, body, and spirit, you can build on it.

CLAIM, BRAG, SHARE 1. List your abilities, strengths, and accomplishments—and don't be modest. List things you do well even if you think they're no big deal.

Include everything, like making a mean barbeque sauce, listening well, remembering to floss, calming situations down, analyzing, dancing, writing, changing the oil in your car, singing, baking cookies, making do with little, raising children, getting to work on time, making silly faces at babies, picking out amazing outfits, or putting your keys in a regular place so you can find them.

Here are some more ideas: Do you knit, play a sport, maintain your sobriety, care for a pet, pay bills on time, take time to chill, or make up new lyrics to songs for your friends' birthdays? Are you fabulous at karaoke? It's like a gratitude list, but about yourself.

Check your list to make sure that lots of things on there *aren't* about what you do for others. If it's mostly about other people, add more things about you. Then share it with at least one other person—or post it on social media or to a group you're in.

_____

_____

_____

_____

_____

_____

_____

_____

<u>CLAIM, BRAG, SHARE 2.</u> Stand or sit like a superhero: hands on your hips or whatever position makes you feel powerful. Using the words "I'm good at" or "I'm great at" (or something like that), say out loud the things you listed above. For example, Lauren would say things like:

- I'm an excellent teacher. (Even as I was writing this, I struggled with what adjective might be "too much"—like, "Is 'excellent' allowed?" "Can I say 'fantastic'?")
- I'm great at parallel parking—I can get into super tight spaces.
- If something's bothering me with a friend, I make sure to talk it through before it becomes a big deal or I build up resentment.
- I went out on my own to do the work I'm passionate about and have successfully supported myself as a self-employed person for more than twenty-five years.

Here's Nadia's list:

- I'm persistent when meeting a challenge. One example: I joined a samba band despite my lack of musical ability and worked hard at it, resulting in years of great fun.
- I'm good at training and taking care of my dog.
- I stay in touch with people and nurture relationships over time and distance.
- I created a beautiful garden.
- I'm willing to be vulnerable.

<u>FAN THE FLAMES 4.</u> Now let's celebrate by writing about the times you've:

- Put the responsibility on an aggressor
- Been angry at an aggressor or those who supported or excused their behavior
- Thought of options while in the middle of a stressful or threatening situation
- Been able to avoid self-blame

_____

_____

_____

_____

FAN THE FLAMES 5. Take one of the stories from Chapter 2. Write everything that the person in the story did—or thought about doing—to advocate for or protect themselves. Include times their intuition or doubt sent them a message.

Then take your own story from Chapter 2. Write everything you did, or thought about doing, to advocate for yourself. Sometimes what you did is notice that you might have done something differently, and that's a step.

_____

_____

_____

_____

_____

SKILL UNDER PRESSURE. If you've been able to handle a difficult situation, you have some of the skills needed for self-defense—quick or creative thinking, action, and calm. Think of a stressful situation you handled or learned from, for example, a medical emergency, a kitchen fire, tension with a friend or coworker, a car problem, a move, a bus that didn't show up when you needed to get somewhere. It doesn't have to be dramatic.

Then write some skills you used or some lessons you learned from dealing with that situation.

_____

_____

_____

_____

_____

_____

TL;DR

- Before we can say what's okay with us and what's not, we need to connect with our feelings, needs, and wants. A coach can help you.

- We learn how to tame the inner critic, treating ourselves with the same kindness and compassion we treat others with. Affirmations are powerful tools for countering negative self-talk and imposter syndrome.

- When we fan the flames of our awareness, our boundary setting, and the times we've asked for what we want, we build our capacity to take action.

THE HEART OF THE MATTER. *What's your main takeaway from this chapter? It could be an idea, an insight, or a new way to say or do something. Write it down, text it to a friend, or draw it. Did you remember one fabulous thing about yourself? Let go of one internal criticism? Celebrate it!*

SELF-CARE BREAK. *Take a deep breath. What self-care will you do now that you've finished this chapter? It can be a small thing (like a few seconds of stretching) or something bigger (like a day off). For more ideas, check in with the plan you made on page xix or the ideas we list on page 10.*

WE SEE YOU! *You're really doing the work now: seeing your habitual thinking and making conscious choices about what comes next. Give yourself a big hug!*

Chapter 7

BECOME AN ACTIVE RESISTER

GROUNDING & CENTERING: Get your move on. Pick a movement that works for your body and do it for one minute (sitting, standing, or lying down):

- March in place.

- Rock your upper body side to side, then forward and backward. Then make circles with your upper body (be sure to switch directions).

- Do a mini cat-cow (from yoga): slowly curve forward, then arch your back with your hands on your lower back.

- Or do any other movement your body likes.

We've talked about how denial, passivity, self-blame, and feelings of low self-worth get in the way of setting boundaries, asking for what we want, and protecting ourselves. That's a lot, but don't despair! In this chapter, we'll address each one of these dynamics with skills and strategies that offer possibilities for transformation.

YOU CAN BE A GOOD PERSON WITH A KIND HEART AND STILL SAY "NO."

Transformations

In this chapter, we'll change:

Denial → awareness, intuition, affirmation of our own perceptions

Passivity → action

Self-blame → anger

Feelings of low self-worth → self-love

Let's take another look at Nadia's thrift-store experience.

Nadia's Story
Going deeper: I couldn't find the words

Nadia went to a thrift store to buy a pair of jeans. There was no dressing room—just an aisle in the back where boxes were stacked.

While she was changing, an employee entered the area, and with his back to her, he began sorting through the boxes. Nadia was uncomfortable *(her feeling)*, but she didn't say anything because he was "just doing his job" *(making excuses for his behavior, denial)* and she didn't want to seem paranoid *(worrying about what he thought of her)*.

He then turned around and asked her how the jeans fit. She dismissed her discomfort *(ignoring her feelings)* and answered him. He then put a tape measure around her waist. Convincing herself *(talking herself out of her feelings)* that he was trying to help her—after all, jeans come in waist sizes—she said nothing but resolved to speak up if he "did anything" *(reacting instead of acting)*. He then put the tape measure around her thigh. Again, she didn't say anything, telling herself that he was trying to get her the best fit.

Finally, he pulled down the jeans and measured her naked thigh. At that point, she was out of excuses for him and out of denial: she was "sure" something was wrong and told him to leave *(set a limit)*. He did.

She felt that the whole assault was her fault *(self-blame)* for continuing to give him the benefit of the doubt *(prioritizing his feelings)*. She didn't tell anyone what happened for a long time because she was sure no one else would be as stupid *(negative self-talk, self-blame)* as she was.

Note how Nadia talked herself out of her feelings, worried more about what he might think of her than about what she was experiencing, and dismissed red flags.

She made excuses for him: he was "just doing his job."

She was worried about making the employee uncomfortable, but paid no attention to her own discomfort and repeatedly dismissed her feelings, convinced herself that he wasn't a problem, and gave him the benefit of the doubt.

Then she blamed herself! That's how powerful rape culture is.

Looking back, she says, "It would've been helpful if I'd asked myself whether he cared about me, about *my* discomfort, or if I'd asked myself what I thought of *his* behavior."

PART 1

Before We Start: Put Yourself First

I THINK OF MYSELF AS HAVING A SINGLE WATERING CAN AND SEVERAL PLANTS, AND SOMETIMES OTHER PEOPLE ASK ME TO HELP WATER THEIR PLANTS, TOO. YOU ONLY HAVE SO MUCH WATER IN YOUR WATERING CAN ON A GIVEN DAY, AND SO YOU HAVE TO DECIDE WHICH PLANTS YOU'RE GOING TO ATTEND TO, AND WHICH YOU CAN'T RESPONSIBLY TAKE CARE OF.

—Angela Chen

Earlier, we talked about how many of us are conditioned to put others' needs before our own.

This isn't all bad. It's wonderful that female conditioning includes nurturing and caring for others. These are positive qualities that all humans could have. What's problematic is when they come at a cost to our own well-being.

To defend ourselves, we need to believe it's okay to take care of ourselves before taking care of someone else. Like we said, we have to be willing to hurt another's feelings (or even their body) in order to protect ourselves. Just like the flight attendants say, put your own oxygen mask on before helping others.

<u>WHERE DO I STAND?</u> Look at the exercise you did on page 73. If there are places you'd like to make yourself more of a priority or take up more space, write them here.

See what you can change to include more time dedicated to things that feed, nurture, or care for you. This list has some categories to get you started, and you're free to add your own.

CATEGORY	WHO COMES FIRST? WHERE AM I ON THE LIST?
Friends	
Family	
Work	
Relaxation: movies, reading, etc.	
Exercise/movement	
Faith	
Neighborhood	
Pets	
Creative life (crafts, writing, etc.)	

CATEGORY	WHO COMES FIRST? WHERE AM I ON THE LIST?
Community involvement/activism	

PART 2

Taking It In: From Denial to Awareness

Transforming denial means:

- Being willing and able to recognize ploys, parting shots, and other red flags
- Trusting your intuition and valuing your perceptions
- Taking action on both of the above.

When we can do these things early on (at the lower end of the spectrum of problematic behaviors on page 16), we have the possibility of interrupting harassment, abuse, or assault before it escalates.

AFFIRMATIVE THINKING. Think of a time when you doubted what you were feeling or seeing. Imagine that you're in a similar situation now, but this time your coach is with you. Write encouragement or affirmations your coach could help you come up with.

_____

_____

_____

_____

_____

_____

PART 3

Get Ready: From Passivity and Reactivity to Action

Remember, it doesn't matter what the other person's intending. If you act, rather than react, you simply state your own feelings or needs and take action to protect yourself. If you focus on yourself, you don't get off course wondering whether someone's intentions are bad.

Rather than being passive, frozen, or reactive in the face of fear, anxiety, or discomfort, you can think actively about what to do to improve your safety. By thinking and being active, you can often creatively and successfully interrupt harassment, abuse, and assault—and survive and heal more easily from any harms you do experience.

Imagine someone grabs your wrist. Your natural reaction might be to freak out: "Danger, danger! They have my wrist!"

The amygdala, the part of your brain that perceives threat and alerts you to it, is just doing its job. But if you can stay connected or get back to your thinking brain, rather than letting the amygdala run the show, your internal dialogue might sound more like this:

"They grabbed my wrist! That's scary! I still have my other hand free, as well as one elbow and both knees and feet. I could hit them with any of those. I also have my voice, and I could yell at them to let me go, or yell for help. Which one do I want to try first?"

The key is to focus on what you _can_ do rather than what you can't. What you _do have_ rather than what you don't. In this way, you can shift the attention from the other person's feelings and needs to respecting your own safety.

Easier said than done, right? Here are some elements to help you be able to assess how threatening a situation is, keep your thinking brain (the prefrontal cortex) online, and make decisions about your safety:

BREATHE. Yes, we keep saying this, but that's because breathing is the number-one way to get or keep yourself grounded, aware, and able to make decisions. Breathing activates your parasympathetic nervous system, which tells the fight-flight-freeze function it's okay to calm down. (You'll learn more about fight-flight-freeze in Chapter 8.)

GROUND AND CENTER IN THE PRESENT MOMENT. Notice what's around you. Think: What would it take for me to get to safety? Rather than freaking out about worst-case scenarios, when you're thinking and in the present moment, you're able to remember and consider options. This relates to the next element, which is . . .

EVALUATE DANGER AND SAFETY. Not all wrist grabs are created equal. Someone grabbing your wrist could be an overexcited coworker telling you a story, a friend fooling around, someone trying to keep you from leaving, someone assaulting you, or anything in between. Now that you've taken a breath, pay attention to the information that lets you know how threatening the situation is, including how far it is to safety.

FINALLY, DECIDE WHAT ACTIONS YOU'LL TAKE TO PROTECT YOURSELF. (In Chapter 8 we'll cover the possibilities in more detail when we talk about Run, Yell, Tell, Hit, and Go Along.)

Obviously, this isn't only about wrist grabs: this is a way to approach any situation in which you feel threatened.

What will they think of me? → What do I think of them?
What will they do *to me*? → What can *I* do?

<u>FLIP THE SCRIPT.</u> In a threatening situation, it can be easy to focus on what the person crossing your boundaries might think of you—or what they might do—if you take an action like leaving or setting a limit. But what do (or did) you think of them?

Pick a situation where you felt uncomfortable or where the other person's behavior was problematic (or use one of the stories from Chapter 2). Maybe you were worried about what they'd think of you if you spoke up. Then flip the script. Answer these questions as yourself or as the person being targeted:

- What did you think of the aggressor and their behavior?
- Were they concerned with your feelings and needs?
- Did they behave in a way you felt was respectful or aligned with your values about how people treat each other?
- What do you think of their behavior now?

_____

_____

_____

_____

_____

_____

_____

_____

Rather than being passive when feeling discomfort or fear, we can think actively about what to do to keep ourselves safe. Thinking about what the other person _might_ do can also get in the way. Instead, try to focus on assessing the situation and on what _you_ can do.

We're not saying it's easy to do things like this, or even to think of them, when you're stressed. That's why it's helpful to practice when you're not being threatened—it'll help you see more options when you are.

For example, think about Nadia's experience in the thrift store. If any of us found ourselves in a similar situation, we might consider:

- Leaving the store
- Telling the employee to stop
- Yelling for help
- Pushing their hand off
- Finding another employee and telling them what was happening
- Calling a friend for support and ideas.

WHAT CAN I DO? Using one of the stories from Chapter 2 or an experience of your own, list options you (or the person being targeted) might have if you face a similar situation in the future.

_____

_____

_____

_____

_____

_____

Lauren's Story
Thinking under stress

I was riding my bike home from work when a young teen started chasing me on his bike. He was trying to intimidate me and literally push me off my bike. I tried using words to get him to leave me alone, but that didn't work.

In my brain I started exploring options: I could sprint to the nearest big street, where there would be plenty of traffic and he'd probably have to leave me alone. I didn't try that because I was in my mid-thirties and he (fourteen or so) could probably out-sprint me. I thought about getting off my bike and facing him with my feet on the ground.

I ended up riding up over a curb (on a road bike!) and up the lawn to the front of a building where someone was having a smoke. I said to the person: "This kid is bothering me—can I stay with you till he leaves?" The teen circled the block probably ten times, but he eventually gave up.

What I took away from that experience wasn't that I found a good solution, even though I did. It was that while I felt threatened, I was still able to think about my options. To me, that's the essence of self-defense.

PART 4

Get Mad: From Self-Blame to Anger

Anger is an appropriate and reasonable response to disrespect and other boundary violations. It's also valuable.

Anger can mobilize us into action despite fear. Fear places us in a passive position. In the moment (or moments) of harassment, abuse, or assault, anger allows us to think about what we can do and tap into energy in order to take action, giving us the power to protect ourselves.

What's more, anger can support healing, as it helps put the blame fully on the aggressor.

Society doesn't see anger that way. It's an emotion to be avoided, denied, or repressed. When BIPOC women, poor and working-class women, or lesbians, for instance, are stereotyped as angry, it's to show that they're not "real" women, because real women don't get angry.

Even more than White women, Black women aren't allowed to get angry without consequences. Black women's bodies, words, emotions, tone, and facial expressions are judged, silenced, policed, and controlled via the stereotype of the angry Black woman. Black women who aren't "nice" and compliant are punished in many ways—from vague disapproval or dismissal to being locked up.

Even when valid reasons to be angry exist, most of society sees our anger as unjustified, and being angry breaks rules about how we're supposed to be, feel, and act.

Sometimes turning anger inward shows up as self-destructive behaviors, such as cutting, eating disorders, addictions, or other harmful coping mechanisms.

FEEL THE ANGER. Take a deep breath—or several. Think about times in your life when someone's crossed your boundaries emotionally, physically, or spiritually. If possible, connect with your anger about the aggressor harming you in that way.

Now write, draw, record, or otherwise create an affirmation (or several) about your right to be angry about what that person did.

MY ANGER HABITS. Think about how you've related to your anger in the past. Were there ways your anger was helpful? Would you do anything differently now? If so, what?

_____

_____

_____

_____

_____

If used well and aimed correctly (at society and at those who harass, abuse, and assault), anger can be a tremendous positive energy source. Write two or more ways you can safely release your anger.

_____

_____

_____

_____

_____

If you feel angry about violence based on race, gender, or other identities, what can you do with that energy? What changes might you focus on working toward? Write some ideas for action. If you've already used anger in these ways, write down how you've done that.

_____

_____

_____

_____

On top of being told not to be angry, we're often pressured to forgive those who harass, abuse, or attack us. Forgiveness can be freeing, but only at the right time and in the right circumstances—and when it's our own choice. Unfortunately, many times we're told to forgive:

- Before we've received support and affirmation for our pain
- Before the aggressor has been held responsible or accountable in any significant way
- Before our needs for healing have been addressed or satisfied.

Being willing to forgive others is characteristic of the stereotypical ideal woman or girl who's compassionate, loving, and forgiving, even while she's hurting. The truth is, we need to forgive ourselves first.

LET GO OF SELF-BLAME. Think of a time you were harassed, abused, or attacked. For this moment, as much as possible, let go of responsibility. Forgive yourself for any choices you made that now feel unwise or things you'd do differently if you had to do it over again. Let go of any shame or self-blame. Put the full responsibility where it belongs: on the aggressor.

Write a sentence in which you release and forgive yourself. For example: "I wasn't responsible for being raped. Wanting to belong didn't mean I wanted to be attacked."

_____

_____

Write another sentence in which you hold the harasser, abuser, or attacker responsible for their behavior and actions. For example, "[Name], I hold you responsible for what you did to me. That wasn't okay. You were wrong to do that."

_____

_____

PART 5

Love Yourself: From Low Self-Worth to Self-Love

[SELF-LOVE IS] A DECISION THAT HAS TO BE MADE FOR SURVIVAL; IT WAS IN MY CASE. LOVING MYSELF WAS THE RESULT OF ANSWERING TWO THINGS: *DO YOU WANT TO LIVE? 'CAUSE THIS IS WHO YOU'RE GONNA BE FOR THE REST OF YOUR LIFE. OR ARE YOU GONNA JUST HAVE A LIFE OF EMPTINESS, SELF-HATRED AND SELF-LOATHING?* AND I CHOSE TO LIVE, SO I HAD TO ACCEPT MYSELF.

—Lizzo

To be able to defend, stick up for, and advocate for ourselves, it's important to believe:

- It's okay to claim my power.
- It's okay to believe in and trust myself, even when I have doubts.
- It's okay to put myself first.
- I can allow myself the same empathy, compassion, and grace I give others.
- My life and safety are precious—I deserve to be safe.
- I am valuable and worth defending.

<u>NO EXCUSE.</u> Look at your story from Chapter 2. Did you use a double standard, making excuses for the other person's behavior in ways you wouldn't for yourself? If so, write your expectations and limits around other people's behavior below and, again, hold the aggressor accountable.

_____

_____

_____

A TALK WITH YOUNGER ME. Many people find that getting in touch with their younger self or inner child helps them treat themselves with more love and care. Imagine yourself as a child or teen (pick any age that feels meaningful to you). Ask the younger you what they're feeling and what they're needing, especially related to the experience you wrote about. Give the younger you attention, reassurance, and comfort; draw or write your thoughts in a notebook so you have them when you need them.

MY OPTIONS. Go to a place (a literal place, or an emotional or imaginary place) where you feel relatively safe. If you feel comfortable closing your eyes, do that. Picking a situation that isn't too intense, think of a time someone crossed your boundaries.

With your coach at your side, imagine yourself taking an assertive action in that situation. Imagine how it plays out so that the outcome is what you want it to be. Your coach can remind you of your rights; they can affirm your abilities and strengths. If doubts creep in or barriers arise, let your coach have their say. They're your ally, and they can help you find options. Write or draw the options you and your coach thought of and what you decided to do.

TL;DR

- We can counter denial with awareness.

- We can change passivity (and reacting to what the aggressor's doing) to active thinking and action, focusing on what we *can* do rather than what we can't.

- We can learn to focus on what we feel, need, want, and think, and act from that rather than from worry about the other person.

- We can transform self-blame into anger at the person (and society) that causes us harm. Anger can help us resist—and heal.

- We can let go of self-blame and learn to love ourselves.

THE HEART OF THE MATTER. *What's the best or most important thing you'll remember from this chapter? What's your favorite way to sum it up? Draw, doodle, tell a friend, record it on your phone, use a journal—anything that works for you.*

SELF-CARE BREAK. *Take a deep breath. What self-care will you do now that you've finished this chapter? It can be a small thing (like a few seconds of stretching) or something bigger (like a day off). For more ideas, check in with the plan you made on page xix or the ideas we list on page 10.*

TIME TO BE KIND. *Be easy on yourself—you're unlearning old ways of being. Along the way, you'll make mistakes! That's okay—mistakes are part of learning. Take a few deep breaths and congratulate yourself for what you've done, no matter how tiny or imperfect it may feel.*

YOU ALWAYS DID THE BEST YOU COULD. YOU'RE DOING THE BEST YOU CAN RIGHT NOW.

Chapter 8

YOU HAVE CHOICES

GROUNDING & CENTERING: Tense and relax. Tense your muscles as hard as you can for ten seconds, then relax them for ten seconds. Take a deep breath, then repeat as many times as you like.

Before and during harassment, abuse, or assault, you may have a chance to stop it. In this chapter, we'll take a deeper look at when those opportunities might come up and offer some options and skills for stopping an aggressor's behavior. These strategies fit into two categories: preventing and interrupting.

We're not promising that these strategies will always work. What we're saying is that though there are no guarantees, they often work.

And knowing more about actions you can take in the future does not mean you did anything wrong in the past. We know you did the best you could, and if you face harassment, abuse, or assault again, you'll have more choices. And if in the future you face harassment, abuse, or assault and you don't use the skills you learned in this book, the responsibility still lies with the person who did it (not you!).

PART 1

Before It Happens: Prevent and Avoid

Let's start here: in a just world, we wouldn't even have to think about taking safety precautions.

Preventing violence has more to do with the aggressors than with what we do or don't do. Prevention ultimately means changing society so that fewer people harass, abuse, and attack to begin with.

Some men are helping other men not only to stop assaults but also to interrupt their peers who are treating others disrespectfully. Meanwhile, empowerment self-defense teachers like Nadia and Lauren are training people targeted for gender-based violence in the skills they need to resist it. Both groups are empowering witnesses or bystanders to take action. We consider *all* these efforts to be essential to creating a society based on respect and trust.

But until the world is safe for everyone, it can be useful to make active choices to lessen the chances of being targeted (remember the self-defense paradox?). This kind of prevention includes:

- Recognizing potential danger and acting to reduce risk and maximize safety
- Making conscious decisions about which actions to take
- Loving yourself enough to take the actions you choose
- Being aware of what's happening—especially of how the people in your life behave, how they treat you and others, and how you feel when you're around them
- Trusting your intuition (even when you're not sure what's happening) and acting on the information it gives you
- Being willing to risk embarrassment, disapproval, or hurting someone's feelings to be safe.

Most prevention tips restrict our freedom and our lives. They sound like "Don't go out alone at night," "Don't leave your drink unattended," and

"Park only in a well-lit area." They also focus on stranger danger, leaving out the more common threats from people we know.

Deciding which measures to follow to increase your safety and what risks to take in order to live freely are very personal choices. As long as you're consciously making these choices, you'll be aware of the risks you may be taking and can be careful in how you do so.

For example, if you listen to music while running, you can run with extra awareness, with only one earbud in, with someone else, where others are around, with a dog, or with the volume turned down. When you get together for the first time with someone you met on an app, you can meet in a public place and share your date's profile with a trusted friend before you go.

Some safety measures may not be things you want to do all the time. You may want to take some actions only if there's a specific problem (like a teacher or boss who says disrespectful things about LGBTQIA+ people or reports of muggings in your neighborhood) or if you feel uneasy with someone (like a date or a street harasser). In those situations, the actions you take can be more empowering than limiting.

Let's look at some examples.

A classmate offered Maya a ride home, which would save her a long subway ride. She felt fine about the classmate and accepted the ride. But she was uneasy about them knowing where she lived and the fact that they might share the info with others. So she asked them to drop her at a nearby store.

Lan, who often modeled for art classes, got a call from Taylor asking them to model for a class. Although there was nothing obviously wrong with the request, and Lan did want the job, they asked about Taylor's reputation at the local community college and took a friend to the class with them.

When Ari was subletting his apartment, his intuition and some inconsistencies in a potential tenant's story made him uncomfortable. So he told them to come when the building manager could "be there to answer questions." The potential tenant never showed up.

Finally, let's not judge others for the choices they make in balancing their own risk and freedom. Almost everything we do carries some risk. Even if someone takes a risk you wouldn't, harassment, abuse, and assault are *always* the aggressor's responsibility.

We SHOULDN'T have to do these things. It's NOT our responsibility. But while we're waiting for the longer-term, bigger change, WE CAN CHOOSE to take action to increase our SAFETY.

MY SAFETY TOOL KIT. List at least three things you already do to keep yourself safe. Here are some ideas from us and our students to get you started:

- If I'm the only person in the gym besides the staff, I leave.
- I keep my keys in my hand when approaching my home or car.
- When I go out running alone, I tell a friend my route.
- When I'm in a new relationship, I take extra care to stay in touch with friends and family and to tell them the pluses *and* minuses of the person I'm seeing.
- When someone I know crosses my boundaries or even just annoys me, I talk it out with them or set a limit before there's a chance for it to get worse.
-
-
-

Now write down any changes you'd like to make to support your safety. They could be concrete: for example, if you have a window without a working lock, you could ask your landlord to put in a new lock. They could be habits: choosing carefully when to allow location sharing on your phone, wearing shoes you can run in, giving your opinion more often, or not leaving most decisions up to your partner. Or they could be setting a boundary or having an overdue conversation about your needs and wants with someone in your life.

_____

_____

_____

_____

You may feel resistance to taking the actions you've written above. For example, you may think, "I should be able to wear whatever shoes I want" or "If I do that, people will think I'm weird, paranoid, neurotic, or rude."

If thoughts like these come up, write down your barriers and then write affirmations or plans to counter them. (As always, writing's only one option. If drawing, doodling, telling a friend, recording it on your phone, or something else is more you, do that!)

THINKING CREATIVELY. When we trust ourselves and are willing to break society's rules, we have many more choices. Here are some examples of situations where awareness, intuition, and creativity can help us stay as safe as possible:

Your car has a flat on a fairly deserted road. You're having difficulty loosening the lug nuts, and there's no cell service. Someone stops and offers help, but they can't get the lug nuts off either. They say they'll drive you to the next town to get help.

Your boss or teacher says they need to meet with you. You know the reasons, and they're valid. They ask to meet at a place and time when the two of you would be alone. They say they know the request may seem odd, and they give an explanation that makes sense. Although you're uncomfortable, you hesitate to offend them.

You've been trying to sell your couch and you need to get rid of it before you move. You finally get a message from someone who's interested and says they need to come right away because they're going out of town tomorrow. You're alone.

You're about to leave work and you don't feel safe on the walk to the bus when it's dark out. A new coworker offers to go with you, but you feel a bit uncomfortable with them for reasons you can't put your finger on.

A neighbor rings your bell on a rainy evening when you are alone. He says he's locked himself out and is waiting for his wife, who should be returning within a half hour. He asks if he could come in for some coffee while he's waiting. You've been uncomfortable around this neighbor because of the disrespectful ways he treats women, although he's been helpful to you in the past when you've had emergencies.

Pick some of these situations and for each one, answer the questions in the table. If you decide you'd do something that feels risky in one of the situations, make sure it's a conscious choice.

SITUATION	WHAT MIGHT I DO TO INCREASE MY SAFETY?	WHAT ARE THE BARRIERS TO TAKING ACTION?	WHAT CAN I DO OR SAY TO MAKE TAKING ACTION EASIER?

The thing about AVOIDANCE is, most of the time, we WON'T KNOW if we prevented abuse or an assault. If we wait to be "SURE" there's a problem, the situation may have escalated or we may have fewer options. Probably all of us have ACTED and AVOIDED or escaped harm and NEVER realized our success.

FAN THE FLAMES 6. Think of a time you changed your route or your plans, said "no," or took another action that may have helped you avoid a boundary violation. To fan the flames of your success, write what you did, whether it was listening to your intuition, recognizing potential danger, or something else. Celebrate your success of taking action.

Be sure to consider times you were aware that something was off, whether or not you took action on it. Just noticing that you *might* have said something is a good thing—and a spark you can fan.

_____

_____

_____

_____

Here are a few examples of actions someone could take in the five situations above. Did you think of others?

- Thank them for their offer and say you want to stay with your car. Ask them to get help for you.

- Let someone know who you'll be with, where you're going, and when you expect to be back—and do it in front of the boss or teacher. Or simply say, "Sorry. That won't work for me." If they ask, "Why not?" just repeat "It really won't work for me. Let's find another time to meet." (That's if you want to find another time to meet. If not, just say the first part.)

- Call someone to come over or be your lifeline. If your intuition's screaming about the prospective buyer's pushiness, give up on the sale. Sometimes you need to put safety first.

- Say, "I appreciate the offer but want to go alone. It would be great if you'd hang out at work with your phone until I get on the bus. If I need you, I'll call."

- Tell him you were just getting ready to leave or you have guests and he can't come in.

- _____

- _____

- _____

PART 2

During: Interrupt + Get to Safety

During harassment, abuse, and assault, we may have the opportunity to interrupt what's happening and get to safety or to reduce the violence and the harm it causes.

In fact, people often use quick thinking, cunning, assertiveness, creativity, and physical resistance to protect themselves, yet for the most part we don't hear these stories. The goal is to escape, survive, and minimize the effect of the violence. It's not to "win."

Actions for this stage include:

- Gaining assertiveness and physical skills to increase your options

- Making conscious choices about what strategies you want to try (including being aware of the ways in which your vulnerabilities and positions of power intersect)

- Developing a mental attitude that allows you to accept whatever choice you make, keeping in mind that choosing to comply is as valid a choice as any other

- Using anger to overcome fear
- Learning skills to de-escalate violence
- Protecting our hearts from any negativity and blame.

It can be tempting to ignore, or pretend not to notice, when someone crosses a boundary, like deadnaming or misgendering you, or "accidentally" touching your breast. There are many reasons you may choose not to say something, among them:

- To avoid embarrassing the person who crossed your boundary
- Because they have power over you
- Because you want them to like you
- Because you're trying to protect your relationship with them.

It's also understandable if you can't or don't act at the first sign of trouble—or ever. Relationships are complicated, the freeze response is real (see page 166), and we often need time to realize what's happening or to understand our options.

Unfortunately, some aggressors take a lack of action as a green light to continue, or escalate, their behavior.

If you choose to respond, you have lots of options. You can use assertiveness (which we'll discuss in Chapter 9). For example, you can use body language like staring, moving away, or removing their hand from your knee. Or you can set a verbal boundary, like "I don't answer personal questions," "If I'm in your way, ask me to move. I don't like being pushed around," "I already told you I don't want another drink," or "Don't contact me ever again."

If the aggressor makes fun of your boundary, pushes back, or otherwise doesn't respect your boundary, that's important information, and it's time to double down.

It's common to worry about what the aggressor will do. If you stay with the thought "What will *they* do to me?" you're stuck. But if you can stay active and think, "What can *I* do?" you'll be able to move through fear to action.

Sorry to say, it's unlikely you'll be able to persuade an aggressor that their behavior's wrong and get them to apologize or promise never to do it again.

(And even if you do get that kind of response, it might not feel genuine to you: abusers often apologize and promise never to do it again; that's part of the cycle of abuse, and it's manipulative.)

As much as we'd love to resolve things through mutual kindness and understanding, other strategies are often needed—and they're often more realistic and effective.

In any self-defense situation, possible strategies come down to these five: RUN, YELL, TELL, HIT, and GO ALONG.

RUN, the first option, may mean running as fast as you can, but it's really anything that gets you out of harm's way. It could be walking, rolling, or driving away. It could be not showing up for a meeting or a date. It could be leaving a relationship or a job. It may mean cutting off contact with a family member. Anything that makes you Not. Be. There. for the harassment, abuse, or assault that's happening (or might happen) can be a successful strategy.

For example, you might:

- Stop engaging with bigoted parents
- End a relationship with an abusive person
- Get out of a ride-share
- Leave a date early
- Refuse to attend a family event
- Stop hanging out with someone you feel uneasy around
- Block someone's number and block them on social media
- Run away from an attacker
- Leave a job that has a toxic boss.

OUTTA HERE. Think of a situation in your life where you've used Run to keep yourself safer, or a situation you'd like to leave, and write it below or in a notebook. Then write what it would take for you to be able to take action (such as becoming more confident about being on your own, a certain amount of money, being willing to hurt another person's feelings, or preparing to retake a class with a different teacher).

_____

_____

_____

_____

_____

_____

YELL, the second option, is using your voice. You'd most likely do this when someone's crossed a boundary with an inappropriate or problematic question, touch, comment, or other action. Often, someone who does that may be testing to see if you'll resist—or if they can continue or escalate the behavior.

Using your voice assertively can reduce the chances of them continuing (see Chapter 9 for assertiveness skills). This can look like talking to the aggressor, telling them what you want, giving them a command, or getting really loud. It can be telling them what's okay with you and what's not, or saying "no."

Speaking up can be difficult, but at the same time, it's simple. And practice makes it easier. Start small, with something like telling your friends what movie you want to watch or asking someone you're staying with for another pillow or blanket. Move up to telling a manspreader on the bus to make room for you, telling a friend how it affects you when they're often late, or asking your hair stylist to change something about a cut that doesn't work for you. Challenge yourself by telling a coworker you can't take their shift or help them with a project.

Literal yelling—the loud kind—can also be powerful and effective if you're in a dangerous situation. Here's how yelling can help:

- It lets the aggressor know what your limit is.

- It can help break the freeze response: if you're yelling, you're breathing, and breathing lets us move through the freeze response (you'll find more on freezing on page 166).

- It can draw the attention of folks around you, which often discourages the aggressor. (A friend of Lauren's was grabbed on the street by a stranger. She yelled loudly, a neighbor turned on a porch light, and the attacker ran away.)

- It can startle the aggressor and discourage them from continuing the attack. (Another friend saw someone approaching him threateningly. He yelled "NO!" really loudly, and the aggressor turned and left.)

Whatever you do to use your voice, be sure to celebrate it. Even if it didn't go the way you planned or have the result you hoped, in speaking up you valued yourself and took action.

MY VOICE. Think of a situation in your life where you've used Yell to keep yourself safer, and write it here.

What would you like to be able to "yell" (loudly or in a regular voice)? Write at least three ideas of your own. Here are some to get you started:

- "I can't listen to you complain about work every day. Please ask me if I have the bandwidth first."
- "Don't touch me without asking."
- "I didn't ask for your advice on using the weight machine. Please leave me alone."
- "Stop expecting me to do all your grunt work/to always take care of you/to do most of the housework."
- "Get your hands off me!"
- "Back off!"

-

-

-

The third option—TELL—is getting help.

This strategy is really underused. U.S. culture is very individualistic, and we get messages that we have to handle everything ourselves.

We get it: most of us find it hard to ask for help. For one thing, we might not get what we ask for. But learning to ask for help is a profound way of honoring and caring for ourselves. And like everything else that asks us to stretch and grow, it gets easier with practice.

Life coach Jamila White says it well: "Your 'I don't need anyone, I'll just do it all myself' conditioning is a survival tactic. You needed it to shield your tender heart from abuse, neglect, betrayal, and disappointment from those who could not or would not be there for you."

You can get help in the moment when something bad is happening—for example, if someone won't stop hitting on you at a party even though you've told them you're not into it, or you're being harassed on the street, or even if you're being attacked.

If you know someone who's around you, like if you're with friends, at work, or at school, you can ask them to stay with you until the aggressor leaves you alone or to join you in telling the aggressor to cut it out.

If you don't know anyone else but other people are around, pick someone and tell them what you need. "You in the red shirt—please go get the bouncer" (or your friend/parent/teacher, or anyone who can help). Identifying the person and giving them a task overcomes the bystander effect, which is the dynamic where the more people who are around when there's a problem, the less likely any one person is to do anything.

Here are two examples of people asking for help.

Mariana's problematic boss asked her to go with them to an isolated area of the workplace. The boss had a reputation for sexual harassment. Mariana asked a coworker to call her and arranged a code that meant she needed help.

Jordan was applying for benefits and the caseworker was indirectly suggesting that he wanted sex in exchange. Jordan had a friend watching their child in the waiting room, and said they needed to remind the friend to give the kid some medication. Jordan then asked the friend to sit in on the interview.

We have to acknowledge the sad, maddening reality that you may not get the help you need. But asking for it increases the chances you will.

(It's also important to get help, or Tell, after a threatening situation is over. For more on that, see Chapter 10, where we talk about how to get support, and the Resources section.)

Of course, there's not always another person around who can help. In those situations, you'll have to rely more on the other strategies: Run, Yell, Hit, and Go Along.

Lauren's Story
At the club

I was at a club and it was so crowded that it felt like we each had about three square inches to stand in. Two people were moving through the crowd, so I squished even tighter to let them pass by. Unfortunately, they stayed there.

This quite-drunk person now had their body pressed up against mine, and all my internal alarm systems were going off. Even though it wasn't a dangerous situation, my amygdala sure felt like it was. I started yelling at the guy (it was very loud in there) to back off and give me space. I yelled at him about five times, and he completely didn't care and didn't respond.

Eventually, I turned to one of my friends (they didn't know what was going on because it was so dark and loud) and asked for help. The friend and I double-teamed the drunk guy, alternating saying things like "Back off" and "Give me some space." He finally got the idea and moved on.

Afterward, I was disappointed in myself for not being able to handle the situation on my own . . . until I realized that I *did* handle the situation—by asking for help!

WOULD YOU HELP ME? When have you used Tell, or asked for help, in setting a boundary or increasing your safety? Maybe you've asked a friend for support, called a hotline, reported someone to HR, or asked someone to walk you to your car.

Sometimes asking for help goes beyond individual action. At one small college library, a male patron was harassing women. Some of the women complained to the administration and were told to be nice to the harasser because "he lacked social skills." Once a few of the women found out that they each weren't the only one being targeted, they asked others to come forward. With so many women complaining together, the college finally acted.

If there are situations you'd *like* to ask for help with, but haven't yet, write your ideas for dealing with them.

If you can't think of examples having to do with boundaries or safety, write down other times you've asked for help (for example, with moving or putting together furniture, reading something over before you turn it in, or getting a ride, etc.).

Should I Yell "FIRE!"?

Lots of people have heard that if they are attacked, they should yell "Fire!" to attract attention. We don't agree. We suggest yelling things like:

- "No!"
- "Stop!"
- "I'm being attacked—get help!"
- "This person is bothering me!"
- "Leave now!"

Why aren't we thrilled with the "yell 'Fire!'" advice? First, remember that 88% of sexual assaults on women and teen girls are by people they know, and at least half of all attacks on men are by people they know (unfortunately, there's no data yet on victim-offender relationships when non-binary people are the ones targeted).

Thus, we're most likely to be attacked on familiar ground: our homes, the homes of our attackers, school, work, and social situations . . . generally inside. If you're in a building and yell "Fire!" most people will run outside, not run *to* the fire. That means yelling "Fire!" can send help away.

Also, yelling serves many purposes. It can attract attention, it reinforces your message, it can discourage an attacker. For the second and third of these, it's more helpful to be yelling something consistent with what you want. If you're defending yourself, or trying to get away, yelling "GET OFF ME!" would be way more effective than yelling "FIRE!"

Before she studied self-defense, Lauren was mugged in the daytime with lots of people around. She yelled "FIRE!" really loudly and no one did anything. So Lauren's personal experience also makes her not a fan of yelling "Fire!"

Of course, we're not opposed to anything that works! (And almost anything might work sometimes.) The most important thing is to yell—and yell loudly.

If you're being physically attacked, you may need to use the fourth option—**HIT**—to protect yourself and make it possible to get to safety. Generally we suggest this if the situation is physically dangerous and you can't Run, Yell, or Tell, or you tried those strategies and they didn't work.

If you need to Hit, you're looking to cause either excruciating pain or temporary disability to make the attacker give up or be unable to continue so you can get to safety. We're looking at targets on the body most of us can reach and injure. You don't have to be an athlete—everyone can learn basic strikes that can get an attacker to stop.

Some of the easiest and most effective ways to hit these targets are with your hands, elbows, knees, head, or feet. If you have crutches or a cane, you may be able to use them to strike; if you have a scooter, walker, or wheelchair, you can ram it into the attacker or run over their feet.

> **I AM NEVER PROUD TO PARTICIPATE IN VIOLENCE,
> YET, I KNOW THAT EACH OF US MUST CARE
> ENOUGH FOR OURSELVES, THAT WE CAN BE READY
> AND ABLE TO COME TO OUR OWN DEFENSE
> WHEN AND WHEREVER NEEDED.**
>
> —*Maya Angelou*

The eyes, nose, throat, groin, knees, and feet are some of the best targets. (Even though movies and TV often show people punching to the stomach and the chest, that's not effective.)

If you go for the groin (and that hurts no matter what body parts the person has), be sure to go up underneath, because that's where the pain is. In addition to the obvious knee to groin, you can kick, you can grab and twist the testicles (if they have them), or you use your hands or an object (for example, a water bottle) to strike.

If you're aiming for a foot (which is a great target because it's almost always available, unlike, say, a groin), stomp down on the instep (where the laces would go if they were wearing shoes with laces) with the whole bottom of your foot (or your cane, walker, scooter, or wheelchair). The instep is also a good target because not much power is needed to injure it—it's mostly about dropping your body weight, or the weight of your mobility device, on them. (To learn more about simple, effective ways to hit, find an empowerment self-defense practitioner at getempoweredbook.com.)

WHAT TO HIT WITH   PLACES TO HIT

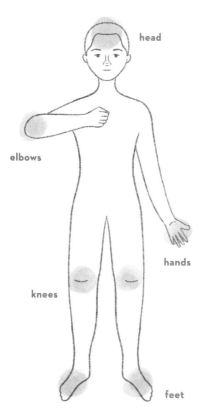
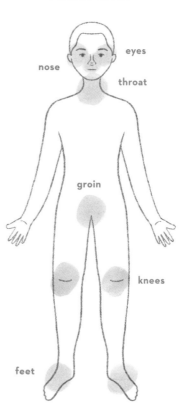

head

elbows

knees

hands

feet

nose

eyes

throat

groin

knees

feet

You've probably felt the effectiveness of some of these, like if you've ever dropped something on your foot or gotten something in your eye. Now imagine someone doing that with lots of power and intention—it hurts!

Lauren's Story
Just like in the cartoons

Once, in a martial arts class, a small, skinny ten-year-old who wasn't hitting hard or on purpose bumped me in the nose with the palm of his hand. It was just like in the cartoons: everything went black, my eyes started tearing, and I literally saw stars!

If my workout partner had been hitting with power and intention, I definitely wouldn't have been able to continue. It reinforced my understanding that the physical self-defense techniques we teach work!

If you've ever done any sports, you know how easy it is to damage a knee. Knees are only made to go one direction, so pressure in any other direction can cause temporary disability, and then the attacker can't run after you.

BIPOC, especially Black and Latina women, trans men, and non-binary people, often are more harshly criticized—and sometimes punished—for using physical self-defense, even when it's justified. If you're BIPOC and physically defending yourself, one thing you can do to increase your chances of being understood to be the defender is to narrate what's happening loudly, shouting things like, "This person's attacking me!" "They grabbed me!" or "They won't let me leave!"

The final strategy, **GO ALONG,** can be a smart choice to reduce the harm you experience and the trauma that goes along with it. This is especially true for very escalated or violent attacks. That's strategic compliance, or "losing to win."

Perhaps the most straightforward situation where going along pretty much always makes sense is in a property attack, where someone wants your stuff, whether it's your phone, wallet, jewelry, bike, car, backpack, purse, sneakers, etc.

Weapons are used in about half of all property attacks, and if you don't turn over your stuff, you're much more likely to see that weapon and have it used against you. There's nothing you own that's worth risking injury or death for.

You might make a similar decision in an attack where they're trying to hurt you (as opposed to taking your property) if you believe or intuit that the safest way to get through it is to go along with it.

Going along, including pretending to be interested, might give you an opportunity to negotiate and reduce harm. You also might be able to change the circumstances to make it possible for you to leave (for example, by going to another room) or to resist. Here are some examples of negotiating during a physical or verbal assault:

- "I'll do what you want. Just let me first go [change my clothes/brush my teeth/take a birth control pill/take out my tampon]."

- "I'm totally into it! Let's just move to the other room so we don't wake the baby."

- "Of course I want to have sex with you. I just need you to put the weapon down first. It's making me nervous, and you totally don't need it."

- "Why do this here? We can go to my place. Just let me make sure no one's home."

- "I'll totally do what you want [stop seeing that friend/skip my sibling's wedding/quit my job/be home before you every night to fix dinner/let you read all my texts] if you stop yelling at me. Can we agree on that?"

- "I'd really like to hear more about what you're saying. I just keep getting distracted when you [threaten me/use insults/wave the knife around]. Could you stop doing that and then I'll listen? I'm sure we can work this out."

Of course, once the person does what you've asked, you don't have to follow through on your promise.

Throughout this book, we're not telling you always to resist an attack. We're simply telling you that you're worth defending and that resistance is generally much, much more effective than we've been told.

You might also pretend to go along until there's a better moment to Run, Yell, Tell, or Hit. Causing a delay also might create an opportunity for someone else to come by and interrupt the abuse or assault.

Sofía's Story
Waiting for a chance

Sofía's abusive ex got her into his car and told her she wasn't going to ignore him anymore. Sofía agreed that he'd "won" and that she'd go and talk with him. After they drove a while, Sofía said she needed a bathroom. He let her out at a convenience store, believing she'd given in, but when she got out of the car she ran inside and got help.

If you make the choice to go along with an attacker, the fact that it's your choice means you keep some of your own power. People who choose to keep themselves safer by going along are less likely to develop post-traumatic stress disorder than those who submit because they feel they have no choice.

If you're being targeted, only you know all the many, many factors going on in the moment: factors such as your relationship to the aggressor, how you're feeling that day, how committed to the attack they seem, how far it is to safety, and so on. So only you can make the decision that's best for you.

When you make the choice to go along with an attacker or abuser, you can still be active. For example, you might be able to get them to put a weapon down, wear a condom, or move to a better location. You might convince them to let you put your child in another room. You might be able to leave evidence, as a woman who put her ring under the seat of the car she was attacked in did. In a relationship where you're being abused, going along might mean physically guarding yourself to reduce injuries—and later reaching out for support or making plans to leave.

No matter what YOU DECIDE to do or what you've done, NO ONE has the right to CRITICIZE your choices. Going along with an assault or abuse isn't the same as consenting. It's a STRATEGY TO SURVIVE with as little harm as possible.

No matter which strategies you use—Run, Yell, Tell, Hit, or Go Along—your goal is to survive with as little harm as possible and to get to safety. Safety can be anywhere: inside or outside, alone or with others, behind a locked door or out in the open, and so on. Very often, safety's where other people are, because attackers usually do their thing in private.

You get to define success for yourself in any situation. Success could be saying what you have to say (even though you can't control how or if the other person hears it or whether they change their behavior). It could be getting to safety. It could be something else.

And Run, Yell, Tell, Hit, and Go Along are strategies, not commitments. Choosing one doesn't mean you're stuck with it forever. As with any strategy, if it's not working, you can try something else.

Fight, Flight, and Freeze

When faced with a threat, our brains and bodies do predictable things. Our brains interpret something as dangerous and dump a bunch of stress hormones into our bodies. Those stress hormones prepare us to fight or run away (the fight-flight response).

This is an involuntary, built-in survival mechanism. And it's helped keep the species alive, preparing us to face, escape, or hide from threats since the beginning of human existence.

You may know what it feels like: your heart rate and breathing speed up, you get sweaty, you might feel nauseated, your vision narrows.

If the threat seems overwhelming and it seems like fight or flight won't be successful, then freeze takes over. Sometimes it lasts only a few seconds, but sometimes it's longer. We may faint or become unable to move, speak, or call out.

And sometimes, to get through an attack or a reminder of past trauma, we'll dissociate—we may feel like we leave our body or we're watching the assault happen to someone else. Like fight, flight, and freeze, this is a survival response; it can protect the consciousness from what's going on.

When all this is happening, the more sophisticated, advanced part of the brain—the prefrontal cortex—goes offline so the body can focus on survival. Without the prefrontal cortex working, we can't reason, plan, communicate, or regulate our emotions.

Having a fight-flight-freeze response doesn't just happen when someone threatens us; it can happen when facing an aggressive dog, an oncoming car, a natural disaster, a person startling us, and much more.

We don't have control over any of these things, but sometimes we can take steps to move out of the fight-flight-freeze response and into conscious action more quickly.

The grounding exercises at the beginning of each chapter are more than good self-care; they can engage the prefrontal cortex and allow you to take action. Other things like doing math in your head or splashing water on your face can as well.

But remember: if you can't take this kind of action, it's not your fault; it's your brain and body doing their survival thing.

Many people, especially those who freeze, judge or blame themselves for their survival response. But it's automatic, it's not in your control, and it's your body trying to keep you safe. So please be kind to yourself about it.

A note about "fawn": many people put fawning in the same category as fight, flight, and freeze. But it's not an involuntary nervous system response. Rather, it's a common strategy for trying to protect ourselves and reduce harm in a threatening situation, and we have a choice whether or not we use it.

TL;DR

- In any self-defense or boundary-setting situation, you probably have options to prevent or interrupt harassment, abuse, or assault. Run, Yell, Tell, Hit, and Go Along are five of them. As the people targeted for violence, we shouldn't have to do these things. It's not our responsibility. But while we're waiting for longer-term, bigger change—for gender-based violence to go away—we can take action to increase our safety.

- Our social programming, or pressure from others, can make it hard to take action (for example, if you worry that people will think you're rude or paranoid). We explore ways to overcome those barriers.

- Fight, flight, and freeze are real, physiological survival mechanisms that we don't have control over. We talk about how they work—and how important it is not to judge yourself for them!

- Remember: no matter what you decide to do or what you've done, no one has the right to criticize your choices.

- BTW: you've probably heard that if you're being attacked, you should yell "Fire!" We have reservations about that and tell you why.

THE HEART OF THE MATTER. *If you were telling a friend about this chapter, what's the main thing you'd tell them? It could be an insight, a skill, or a new way to think about something. Write it down, text it to a friend, or draw it—however you want to reinforce it is good.*

SELF-CARE BREAK. *Take a deep breath. What self-care will you do now that you've finished this chapter? It can be a small thing (like a few seconds of stretching) or something bigger (like a day off). For more ideas, check in with the plan you made on page xix or the ideas we list on page 10.*

TIME TO CELEBRATE. *Now that we've talked about preventing and interrupting harassment, abuse, and assault, you might see some of the steps you've taken to protect yourself in a different light. You're rewriting the script of your life with new skills and new understanding. Celebrate what you've learned, changed, and understood so far—and hold yourself with kindness.*

I HAVE THE RIGHT TO SAY "NO."

Chapter 9

GET YOUR MESSAGE ACROSS

Speak Your Mind—and Your Heart

GROUNDING & CENTERING: Tap your way to calm. You can do this exercise with the movements described, or imagine them in your head; either way can be helpful. Hold one arm out and with a gentle, open hand on your other arm, tap along your first arm, going up the outside of your arm (from hand to shoulder) and then down the inside (armpit to palm). Switch arms and do the same thing. Then tap the outside and inside of your legs, chest, belly, and lower back. Finally, use the tips of two fingers to tap the small muscles of your face, like under your eyes, above your brow, under your nose, and on your cheeks. When you're done, shake it out!

Once you know that something isn't working for you—or there's something you want—assertiveness (aka boundary setting or verbal self-defense) is usually the best strategy to communicate that. We'll break down the ways you can do that here and offer some opportunities to practice.

Some situations, such as dealing with an abusive partner, might call for other strategies like de-escalation, negotiation, pretending to go along while keeping yourself as safe as possible, and making plans to get help. (For more on de-escalation, see page 208.)

PART 1

What Is Assertiveness?

ASSERTIVENESS is saying what you feel, need, or want directly, clearly, and respectfully—without hinting, apologizing, expecting someone to read your mind, or being passive-aggressive. Being assertive also means no name-calling, put-downs, or cursing.

By being assertive, we take responsibility for our own feelings and don't guess someone else's motives. *Assertive* means respecting our own rights *and* the rights of the other person.

Women and BIPOC men are often seen as being aggressive when we're simply being assertive. Assertive behaviors and speech are usually celebrated or rewarded in White men (especially White cis men); they're seen as signs of leadership, making the person high status, ambitious, knowledgeable, or dominant—all of which are seen as positive traits. In women and BIPOC men, those same behaviors and speech are viewed as bossy, abrasive, unattractive, ambitious (the same thing but now it's bad!), brusque, bitchy, or threatening—and, for femme people, the death knell: unlikeable. All this amounts to more pressure to avoid setting limits or asking for what we want. But we need assertiveness as one of the tools in our toolbox for clear communication and for safety.

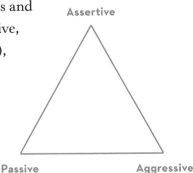

How is being assertive different from being passive, aggressive, or passive-aggressive?

WHEN WE'RE PASSIVE, we don't advocate for ourselves. We agree with things that we really don't *want* to agree with—ignoring our own feelings, needs, and wants to put other people first. We don't voice our opinions.

Although there are definitely times to put other people and their feelings first, we're passive when we do it as a habit, without thinking about it, or going against our own feelings, needs, and wants. We avoid confrontation or even negotiation because we can't tolerate conflict. We cave and don't respect our *own* rights, or we don't think we—or our needs—are as important as others'.

Agreeing to do someone a favor when you really wanted to spend time doing something else—or nothing—is an example of being passive. When someone asks what show you want to watch or where you want to eat and you answer, "I don't care. Whatever you like," even though you do have a preference, that's also passive.

You may even agree to a date—or to sex—because you don't want to hurt someone's feelings or because it's easier than saying "no" or continuing to say "no." You find it harder to set limits than to just go along.

This way of dealing with the world makes it easier for aggressors to escalate their boundary violations.

Let's be clear: no matter what you do or don't do, the harassment, abuse, or assault is entirely the aggressor's responsibility.

WHEN WE'RE AGGRESSIVE, we're on the attack. We accuse someone else, assume the worst motives for their actions, or intrude on their space. Pointing a finger in someone's face, ridiculing them, or using curse words or put-downs are acts of aggression. When we're acting aggressively, we aren't respecting other people's rights.

Some of us react aggressively when we feel we're disrespected. It can be difficult to refrain from retaliating.

But aggression, including verbal violence, can escalate situations as each person responds to the other by attacking back.

Many people confuse aggression and escalation with being strong. But the truth is, if someone can set you off with phrases like "your mother" or "bitch," or if they can provoke you with actions like bumping into you or showing up without letting you know first, *they're* in control of *you.* Because you react predictably when provoked or challenged, you give up your power to them.

If you tend to default to aggression, ask yourself whether you're in control when you do so.

WHEN WE'RE PASSIVE-AGGRESSIVE, we don't want to do or agree to something, but instead of saying that (which would be assertive), we:

- Procrastinate
- Give someone the silent treatment
- Do the thing badly
- Disguise criticism as "compliments" or "jokes"
- Pout or whine
- Avoid the person or avoid talking about the issue
- Purposely "lose" something important to the other person or the task
- Forget or pretend to forget
- Keep score
- Make excuses
- Blame someone else
- Say everything's fine when it's not.

Women, White women especially, may choose this approach because it's a more culturally approved way of trying to get their needs met.

Situations exist when acting either passively or aggressively can be a strategic, useful choice temporarily to achieve an end. But these need to be conscious choices. As a habit, we're far better off—and safer—if we cultivate assertiveness.

Three Ways of Communicating, and How to Tell the Difference

PASSIVE	AGGRESSIVE	ASSERTIVE
Gives up space	Takes another's space	Maintains their own space
Often results in frustration, defensiveness, impatience, resentment, and increased aggression from the other person	Tends to escalate situations	Can increase safety and make relationships healthier
Works to avoid conflict; tries to keep the peace at a cost to themselves	Focuses on the other person; attacking or blaming	Sets limits respectfully; uses "I" statements to take responsibility for their feelings
Says whatever they think the other person wants to hear	Uses name-calling and blaming; says things like "You always . . . ," "You never . . . ," and "The trouble with you is . . ."	Says things like "I feel . . . ," "I need . . . ," and "I want . . . "

Example: INTRUSIVE QUESTIONS		
Answers all questions, goes along with the conversation, or evades the questions	*"You're so nosy. You're always getting into people's business."*	*"Please stop asking me personal questions. I won't answer anymore."*

Example: UNWANTED TOUCHING		
Ignores the touching or tries to shrug the other person's hand off	*"Get your ugly paws off me. You are one of the most obnoxious people I've ever met. No wonder no one likes you."*	*"Hey River. I told you I don't like you touching me. Cut it out."*

Example: CUTTING IN LINE		
Lets the other person in line and feels victimized and resentful	*"What's your problem? What the &%*# do you think you're doing?"*	*"I've been waiting and you just cut the line. You need to wait like everyone else."*

PART 2

Get Your Assertive On

You're probably saying, "Okay, assertiveness sounds good, so how do I do it?" That's what the rest of this chapter's about, and you'll have a chance to practice each skill along the way.

Elements of Assertiveness

- Take up space with your voice, body, and face.
- Tell the other person what you want them to do.
- Be direct: avoid excuses, explanations, and apologies.
- Name the behavior.
- Stay on your own agenda.
- Repeat yourself and get more intense.

TAKE UP SPACE WITH YOUR VOICE, BODY, AND FACE

You may have heard that the words you say make up only one-third of what's communicated; two-thirds of communication is nonverbal. So your tone, body language, and facial expression are just as important as the words you say in getting across a clear, confident message.

These nonverbal ways of communicating also are part of how you use space. They send a message showing how you feel about your right to exist in this world. They can either convey a firm belief in your rights or send a message of anxiety and apology. Taking up space doesn't mean taking over anyone else's; it simply means taking up your rightful share.

It's important to look serious with your voice, body, and face because if any part of you isn't serious, it can undermine your message. For example, smiling while you say "no," having your voice go up at the end of a sentence ("You need to stop?"), or tilting your head can make your message less clear or firm. Try keeping your face serious, your voice steady, and your head level. If it helps, think of someone who intimidates you a bit and try to channel their energy.

Project confidence by holding a steady gaze. You don't have to look the other person in the eye. Just make sure your eyes are up and your face is facing theirs. That might mean looking at their forehead, chin, or ear. Or you can look right past them, over their shoulder.

Eye contact often signals confidence, but because it means different things in different cultures (for example, in some cultures it's rude) and in different contexts (in some, it can be flirtatious; in some, it can be a challenge), only you know whether to make eye contact in a specific situation.

PASSIVE AGGRESSIVE ASSERTIVE

USE A FIRM VOICE

Think of a stern parent or teacher when they're annoyed or telling a child what to do. Or think of how you talk to a toddler or a dog when they're doing something dangerous. "STOP!" is probably the way you'd say it.

Your voice is strong and unwavering—the word *stop* doesn't come out as if it has more than one syllable or change notes. It doesn't mean you have to shout, though sometimes you might—it just means you're serious. You can be quiet and very, very serious.

POSE LIKE A SUPERHERO

In general, the goal when being assertive is to take up space. Put your feet apart, make your spine as straight as you can, and keep your hands free (not in your pockets, not behind your back). You don't have to be standing; you can totally do this sitting down and turn your chair or scooter to face them. Think Wonder Woman, except you don't have to have your hands on your hips. Your body sends the messages "I've got this!" "I'm in charge!" and "I know what I'm doing!"

In more threatening situations, you'll want to have your hands up if you can. These "stop sign" hands reinforce your verbal message of setting a boundary. Keep your arms bent so they're ready to protect your head if the person tries to hit you. Another benefit of keeping your arms bent is that they're harder to grab.

ASSERTIVE   ASSERTIVE   ASSERTIVE

KEEP YOUR FACE SERIOUS

A serious expression is key, and the biggest challenge can be a nervous smile. If someone's pressuring or threatening you, you're probably going to feel nervous, and for a lot of us that shows up as a smile.

Smiles can smooth social interactions and make the world more pleasant. But it takes effort for many of us to smile only when we want, because in addition to the nervous smile, women in this culture are expected to smile, and we often get negative reactions when we don't.

Women of color, especially Black women, are criticized for seriousness even more than White women are—think of the stereotype of the angry Black woman—and Black women's interactions are judged and limited because of it.

Our faces and feelings are our own. Ideally, we'd smile only when we felt like it. But for many of us, it's a habit.

The stern parent or teacher is a good model here too. Remember when you were little how someone in authority could get you to "behave" just by giving you a look? That look is what you're going for.

There are lots of strategies for wrangling that smile if it creeps up on you. Try these.

<u>AM I SMILING?</u> For the next day or two, take special notice of when you smile. When is it automatic and when is it a choice? One way to find out is to decide to *not* smile for a day. A choice *to* smile is meaningful only when you also have the choice *not* to do it. See what you notice and write it here.

When I don't smile, I feel . . .

_____

If your feelings when you don't smile are painful or anxious, write an affirmation about your right to choose when to smile. Write or draw as many of these as you want to cover all your feelings for that day.

GET SERIOUS. If you find yourself smiling when you're nervous, be kind to yourself. It's common. To get a serious face, the number-one strategy is to take a deep breath. Try that a few times and see if you can get comfortable with it.

Other ideas:

- Think of someone who seriously pisses you off.
- If you have any theater or acting training, enlist that.
- Pretend to be confident even when you're not. Fake it till you make it.
- Look *past* the head of the person you're talking to, maybe over their shoulder. Don't look right at their eyes or even their face. This can help reduce stress.

Experiment and notice what makes your nervous smile get serious. When you find something that works, hang on to it.

PUT IT ALL TOGETHER. Pay attention: Do you use a level tone, without rising at the end of a sentence? If you're introducing yourself in a group, can others hear your name?

Be aware of your body language when you sit, stand, and move. As much as possible, are your arms free, or do you tend to keep your hands in your pockets, folded in front of you, or behind your back? Is your posture firm and balanced? If you use a mobility device, do you take up space with it, especially as you move?

Is your head up or do you look down, avoiding eye contact? (Remember Lauren's story about looking down in Chapter 1?) As much as possible, do you sit or stand tall, or do you slump? Can you identify times when you're likely to take up little space (looking down, slouching, apologizing for the space you take up)?

Now write, draw, tell a friend, or record into your phone the answers to these two questions:

1. What are your areas of strength?

2. What areas would you like to work on?

"NO" GAME 1. If your default is "yes"—and for many of us it is—it's super important to have "no" as part of your vocabulary. If you're always reacting to others and their needs, even their unspoken ones, there's little or no space for yourself, your wants, and your needs.

With a trusted friend, take turns being the person saying "no" and the person asking the questions. The "no" person can only use that word—no apologies, explanations, or alternative solutions. The person asking questions should use a variety of questions, ranging from emotionally simple to difficult, lighthearted to loaded. And the person asking questions backs off when they hear "no."

If there's no one you feel comfortable practicing with, on the following page you can write a dialogue back and forth, or play both roles out loud, or anything that gets you in an exchange like this.

Use these examples or make up your own.

Can I: Borrow your pen? Have a drink from your water bottle? Leave my kids with you while I run to the store? Use you as a reference? Speak to the group without using the microphone? Use your phone? Stay with you tonight? Borrow your toothbrush? Copy your homework? Tag you in this photo? Touch your hair? Take my mask off in your room? Just this once make a dinner reservation at this place with steps? (I'll help you up the steps, I promise.)

Will you: Have sex with me? Take my picture? Cover my shift? Give me your notes from class? Make me lunch? Lend me money? Come to my house after work? Save my seat? Share my post?

Set a timer and do this for one minute per person.

We know that in real life you might choose to say more than "no," but this is an exercise to help you get more comfortable with "no" and see what feelings come up when you say it.

When you're done, write below or talk with your friend. How did it feel to say "no" to some of those requests? Did you have an impulse to say "yes," or to apologize or explain?

Many of us do, because we've been taught to be "agreeable" or "nice," or to avoid hurting people's feelings. How do you feel when you're not following your Nice Girl training?

You can also practice in your head. Think of a time you said "yes" when you really wanted to say "no." It could be a time you helped someone study for a test or helped a coworker with a task, shared your password, lent a friend or family member money, or listened to a friend complain about their partner for the fourth time this week—but you didn't want to.

It could be a time you had sex you felt pressured into or did something during sex that you didn't want to.

Take a deep breath, explore what you feel, need, and want, and then say out loud something like "No, I can't," "I'm not okay with that," or "That won't work."

Although practicing these kinds of interactions can be uncomfortable, we do have a reason for it: the goal is to help us get used to saying "no," be able to anticipate the feelings that might show up about it, and prevent those feelings from getting to us.

Shana's Story
Definitely not a morning person

Shana's not a morning person, and she doesn't drink coffee. Yoga is pretty much the only productive thing that she enjoys doing before 9 a.m. But she often does early meetings because even though she's on the West Coast, most of her co-workers are on Eastern Time.

One day, someone suggested 8 a.m. Pacific Time as their only available meeting time and, as an experiment, Shana politely declined. *And they magically found another time.*

Shana said: "This was yet another lesson on how to take care of myself first, instead of defaulting to caring for others and putting my needs last."

I MEAN IT! Get in front of a mirror. Take a deep breath, and with a strong and serious voice, body, and face, say "Stop!" Try a low-key "Stop" for annoying situations, a medium "Stop!" for more problematic situations, and a loud "STOP!!!" for dangerous situations. Say lots of levels of "Stop," louder and softer—and extra loud. Having the ability to really yell can help you attract attention if you're in a dangerous situation.

After you've done it on your own, you can graduate to saying boundaries out loud to videos of YouTubers or news anchors (it's harder than saying it in front of a mirror, but you're not yet practicing on live humans). Finally, gather a friend or two and practice with them—it's different with real people in front of you.

"I" Statements
An important assertiveness tool

"I" statements are a way to state what you feel, need, and want in which you take responsibility for your feelings and don't accuse the other person.

"You" statements, especially those that start with things like "The trouble with you is...," "You always...," or "You never...," won't get you what you want.

All "I" statements include saying what you feel in response to someone else's actions. Here are some examples.

When you _____, I feel _____. Please _____.

I feel _____ when you _____ because I _____.

I would like _____.

Let's look at one situation and some ways you could use "I" statements.

- "When you keep pressuring me for sex, I feel scared and disconnected. Please drop it when I tell you I'm not into it right now."

- "When you keep pushing me for sex, I feel hurt. I need to know you care what I want too. I'd like it if you'd check in with me and consider how I feel."

- "I'm upset that you're pushing me for sex when I said 'no.' I'd like both of us to listen when the other person says they don't want to have sex at a particular time. It's okay with me to talk about it. It's not okay to pressure me when I've made it clear I don't want sex."

Note: saying things like "I feel you're totally inconsiderate of other people" isn't an "I" statement. "I" statements refer to actual *feelings* (not your judgments or interpretations of the other person's motives or actions) and a personal point of view, like: "I'm offended that you keep telling racist 'jokes.' I've told you I don't like to hear them."

TELL THE OTHER PERSON WHAT YOU WANT THEM TO DO

Assertiveness usually comes down to telling the other person what you want them to do.

Sometimes when someone crosses a boundary, we get so scared/angry/confused/flustered/surprised/horrified/shocked/nervous/humiliated that we can't think of what to say. "Tell them what you want them to do" helps us figure that out.

Depending on your relationship with the person and the situation, what you say may be:

- Simple: "Get away from me!"

- More complex: "When you come home and spend your time watching TV and on your phone, I don't feel connected. I feel lonely and my feelings are hurt. I want you to set aside fifteen minutes a night for us to talk and be together."

- In between: "This isn't the best route. Here's how I'd like you to go."

Telling someone what you want is the number-one element in setting a limit. Think back to when we talked about tuning into what you feel, need, and want. Remember how we practiced checking in with how we feel and figuring out what we need, and then what we want? When you get to the "want" part of it, that will help you know what to say. "I want you to . . ." sentences can be as varied as you and your challenges.

For example, if you want them to stop touching you, the sentence is "Stop touching me."

Use statements, not questions. "Leave me alone," not "Would you please leave me alone?" or "Leave me alone, okay?"

Polite words such as *please* are helpful in some situations, like if you're setting a limit while trying to preserve a relationship or if you think your limit will be more likely to be heard if you use words that signal politeness or respect. But if the person doesn't listen to you and you need to say it again, leave out the *please* and other polite words.

Same with saying things that soften your limit. If you want your boundary to land gently or you're prioritizing the relationship over your needs at the moment, waffling phrases like these can be helpful:

- "I can't talk to you *right now*."
- "You know I really don't want to talk. *It's not personal*."
- "I need to tell you something. I really need some alone time. *I hope that works for you*."
- "This isn't *a good time* for me to talk."
- "No hugs *today!*"

If you really mean no hugs *ever* or "I don't want to come over *for the rest of my life*," you don't do anyone any favors and you don't increase your safety by adding phrases that soften your meaning.

If the other person doesn't respect your limit, then it's time to repeat yourself with the waffling phrase edited out, for example: "I want to be left alone" or "Leave me alone."

And remember, you can always change your mind. Even if you've said "yes" to something, you can always change to "no," and even if you've done something before, you can say "no" to it this time or next.

<u>REAL-WORLD EXPERIENCE.</u> Take your assertiveness out for a test drive in the real world. Practice saying "no" more often in your life and only saying "yes" when you *really* want to. Start by saying "no" to at least one thing a day, then two. Say "no" to something you'd usually say "yes" to but that you really don't want to do. Maybe helping a coworker or a neighbor, volunteering for something at your child's school, or running an errand for your partner fit into that category.

You can also pause before saying "yes." Give yourself a thirty-second, fifteen-minute, two-hour, or twenty-four-hour waiting period. Agree to do things only when you want to and have the bandwidth.

Putting a sticky note (paper or virtual) on your phone, laptop, mirror, dashboard, or refrigerator can help you remember to pause rather than automatically agreeing to something.

If you can't say "NO," your "YES" isn't real.

BE DIRECT: AVOID EXCUSES, EXPLANATIONS, AND APOLOGIES

"No" is a complete sentence. You don't need to explain yourself. You don't need to apologize for how you feel or what you want. You also don't have to wait for your "turn" in the conversation—if someone isn't respecting you or your boundaries, go ahead and interrupt them. They've forfeited their right to politeness.

In some low-key situations, you might want to start with an apology or explanation (for example, "I'm sorry. I don't share my water."). But if the person persists, they're not respecting your "no," and you'll want to drop the niceties.

It can be difficult to refuse to give an explanation, because explaining is considered polite. At the same time, being asked to explain ourselves can imply that our wishes themselves aren't valid.

Excuses and explanations also can backfire as they give the other person an opening. Here are some examples.

> You say: "I can't talk to you now. I have to get to the babysitter's."
> They might say: "Oh, that's no problem. My car's around the corner. I'll give you a lift."

> You say: "I can't go out tonight. My parents won't let me."
> They might say: "Oh, don't worry. We'll tell them I'm your TA and they won't mind."

> You say: "I don't want to have sex—I'm on my period."
> They might say: "That doesn't bother me. Let's do it."

Along with not needing to explain, we also don't have to apologize for our feelings, requests, opinions, desires, or being. A lot of us have a bad case of the sorrys. Of course, small apologies smooth everyday interactions—say, if two people start to walk through a doorway at the same time. And big apologies are necessary if you've done something wrong or act from somewhere other than your best self.

But you don't need to apologize to someone who bumps into you or say "I'm sorry, but I think . . ." or regret saying what you want. Look at this list, and add your own.

I Don't Need to Apologize For:

- Asking for something
- Choosing what works for me
- Choosing who I want in my life
- Having feelings (being happy, sad, angry, upset, etc.), wants, and needs
- Needing accommodations or protecting my health
- Not being perfect
- Putting myself first
- Saying "no"—or saying "yes"
- Speaking up or standing up for what I believe in

- Taking time for myself
- Taking up space
-
-
-

SWEAR JAR

SAYING "I'M SORRY" UNNECESSARILY JAR

<u>AM I SORRY-ING?</u> Pick an hour, afternoon, day, or week to track when you say "sorry" or otherwise apologize when you don't need to. Choose a time you'll be around other people.

As much as you can, notice every time you say "sorry" or something similar. Do you say "sorry" when someone bumps into you or is in your way? Do you say "sorry" at the beginning of sentences to ease your way into the conversation?

Next, practice saying, "I'm not sorry" every time you catch yourself apologizing for no good reason. If you're with a close friend, tell them you're trying to break the sorry habit, and say it out loud. If you're in a situation where it might not be a good idea to say your anti-apology, such as at work, practice yelling, "I'm not sorry!" inside your brain.

FAN THE FLAMES 7. Noticing is the first step to change. If you've ever stopped yourself from saying "sorry" when you didn't need to, write it down now so that you can build on it.

_____

_____

_____

_____

_____

Now write (or draw, doodle, or record) what your options would be if you were in a similar situation in the future.

NAME THE BEHAVIOR

Often, aggressors disguise their behavior to look like something more innocent. For example, someone may pretend they're interested in what you're reading or what game you're playing. Both of you know that isn't what they're really interested in. If you don't want to have the conversation, take steps to end it. Don't pretend that the book or the game is the point. Break the silence by naming what's happening.

You may be very direct or you may choose to start out with humor or another "softer" approach. ("Hmmm. Somehow, I have the feeling you aren't really interested in my game . . .") If the person persists, be more direct. ("I don't want to talk.")

If someone doesn't respect your boundary, you may want to name the behavior (naming the behavior is in italics). Here are some ways that can sound:

- "I told you I don't want to talk to you. *Now stop harassing me.*"
- "I made it clear I don't want a drink. *Stop pressuring me.*"
- "I've told you I'm not comfortable with your arm on my shoulder. *Stop ignoring what I said.*"
- "What's the deal here? I told you to stop. *You're not listening.*"

Naming the behavior can make someone stop. One person Nadia knows was being pressured for sex and didn't consent. The aggressor kept making excuses and gaslighting Nadia's friend. So her friend said, "I said stop. If you keep doing this, this is rape and you are a rapist." The aggressor was shocked because they didn't see themselves that way—and stopped.

One thing all these examples have in common is that you're telling the other person what they're *doing* that you don't like ("You're standing too close") rather than judging them as a person ("You're such an asshole").

Be specific so that they know what behavior to change and so that you can tell if they've changed. This means saying things like "You're asking personal questions. Please stop" rather than "You're being disrespectful" or "I don't want to talk."

Avoid cursing, name-calling, put-downs, and anything else that could unnecessarily heat up the situation.

STAY ON YOUR OWN AGENDA

Once you know what you want the other person to do (the "want" in "I want you to"), that's your agenda. After you've said it (for example, "Stop calling me" or "No more questions about my dating life" or "If you keep making comments about my weight, I'll leave"), don't respond to diversions, threats, questions, blaming, guilt-tripping, gaslighting, or any other manipulations someone sends your way. Just stick to what you want.

Imagine yourself saying something like "Please stop talking about my body. Let's concentrate on work." If the person doesn't listen to you, you might make that "I need you to stop talking about my body." These are the polite, yet still assertive, versions.

But when someone doesn't respect your limits, they often push back. You might hear some variation on "I'm just giving you a compliment. Why do you have to be so sensitive?"

To stay on your agenda, don't engage. Chances are they understand exactly what you're asking for but are seeking to undermine your feelings by pushing you to explain or second-guess yourself. Just repeat yourself: "Stop talking about my body." No matter what they say, don't get derailed. You might change your wording slightly if they continue to push back: "I asked you to stop."

It can sometimes be effective to turn it around and ask them to explain why they can't honor your request: you can say something like "I asked you to stop talking about my body. What's the reason you won't stop?"

REPEAT YOURSELF AND GET MORE INTENSE

In general, unless it's obvious that the aggressor plans to attack you, being firm yet gentle is a good way to start. If the other person disregards your wishes or discounts or ridicules you, it's most effective to repeat yourself and get more intense.

Repetition can get a person to stop what they're doing. If you set a limit or tell them what you want, and they refuse to honor it, that gives you important information about them and their intentions.

So you can simply repeat yourself in the same way ("Leave me alone." "Leave me alone." "Leave me alone." "Leave me alone."). Or you can repeat yourself and get more forceful with your voice, body, and facial expression ("Please leave me alone." "I asked you to leave me alone." "Leave me alone!" "LEAVE NOW!").

Don't give them an opportunity to say anything back, and don't respond to anything they do say.

CONTROLLING TALK. As you know, aggressors often try to take control of the conversation and get you away from your agenda. We talked about this kind of pushback, especially parting shots, in Chapter 3. Here are a few more. Put a check next to the phrases that sound familiar or that someone's used to try to control you. If certain types of pushback especially get to you, circle them. If you have any others that get to you, add them to the list.

- ☐ "You let me last time."
- ☐ "[Someone else] said it was okay."
- ☐ "You need to relax."
- ☐ "What's your problem?"
- ☐ "I thought you liked me."
- ☐ "You're hurting my feelings."
- ☐ "It's just a compliment."
- ☐ "You know you like it."
- ☐ "Excuse me for trying to be nice. I guess it's a crime to be friendly."
- ☐ "Are you on your period?"
- ☐ "You're the only one who can help me."
- ☐
- ☐
- ☐
- ☐
- ☐

"NO" GAME 2. Using the same questions as in the "no" game on pages 181 and 182, we're going to practice saying "no" with pushback. Ask your friend to keep going after you say "no" and to say some of the things on the list above or any other kind of pressuring statements or questions you've heard before.

Your job is to continue to say "no," no matter what they say.

In real life, if the other person pushes back, you can simply repeat yourself ("That doesn't work for me") or say something like "It just doesn't" or "Trust me, it doesn't" or "I'm not going to go into it. Like I said, it won't work."

"NO" GAME 3. Again, your friend is going to ask you questions, you're going to say "no," and they're going to push back. Have them ask you and push back at least two or three times before they give up. When they do give up, they're probably going to say a parting shot.

If you don't have anyone to practice this with, you can write a back-and-forth dialogue, play both roles out loud, or do anything that gets you into an exchange like the ones above.

Although practicing these kinds of interactions can feel pretty awful, it does have a purpose: to help us get used to parting shots, be able to predict them showing up, and be able to let them go by without distracting us from our agenda.

"NO" GAME 4. For the final round of the "no" game, we're adding touch. Ask a person you trust to put a hand on your shoulder. Tell them to take their hand off you; they should then take it off. Do that a few times and see how it feels. Also, if there's anything you want to work on, like a strong voice or a serious face, practice that.

Then make it harder and more like real life. When you say, "Take your hand off me," have them use their own words or some of the lines on page 193 to push back on your boundary and keep their hand on your shoulder. You should simply repeat your command.

Then, as you repeat yourself and get more intense, take their hand firmly off your shoulder and give it back to them. This is using your body to reinforce your message. You have power over their hand.

While you're doing this, be aware of how you feel about stating your wants and staying on your agenda.

Remember, you can always take a break or ask your friend to stop the exercise. Be sure to breathe. And if you feel emotions or sensations coming up, make a note of them so you can think, draw, write, or talk with a friend about them.

TAKE YOUR HAND OFF ME!

Keep the focus on what you want and need and on *the aggressor's* behavior. Don't get hooked by their diversions and attempts to focus on what's "wrong" with you.

Again, if there isn't someone you feel okay doing this with, practice it out loud or in your head—it'll still be helpful.

OTHER TOOLS FOR ASSERTIVENESS

Here are some other tools that may help you be more assertive.

USE LEAD-IN LINES

Since the hardest part of a journey can be the first step, when it feels difficult to assert yourself, it can be helpful to use a lead-in line that commits you to finishing your statement. Look at these lead-in lines in italics:

- *"You know what?* I don't like you touching me without asking if it's okay."

- *"I need to tell you something.* If you expected something in return for doing me a favor, you needed to make that clear earlier."

- *"Listen to me for just a minute.* I'm offended at the comments you are making about [women/BIPOC/LGBTQIA+ people]."

GO BACK LATER

All of us are sometimes caught off guard and don't say anything about offensive speech or behavior. We might have a chance to go back and say something later. Even if you didn't say anything at the time, this shows the other person that you're willing to speak up and that you consider your feelings and rights important.

Here are two examples:

- "Dr. Williams, on Tuesday, when you started to do a breast exam even though I came in for a sprained ankle, I didn't say anything because I was shocked. What you did was unprofessional and offensive. You didn't explain to me why you were doing it, and you didn't ask my permission first."

- "I'd like to talk with you about the other day. I didn't say anything at the time, but I want you to know I was very uncomfortable with that 'joke' about [BIPOC/women/LGBTQIA+ people/etc.]. It's not acceptable to me, and it's especially offensive in a work environment."

Another way to go back later is to write to the person, detailing what they did, how you felt about it, and what you want them to do now.

IMAGINE YOU'RE PROTECTING SOMEONE ELSE

Many people, especially those raised female, find it easier to speak up for others rather than themselves—even more so if the ones who need speaking up for are children. You can use this strategy to build your assertiveness muscle or be an upstander who helps people who are being targeted—and you'll help make the world a better, more respectful place.

Think about a time you saw someone being mistreated or disrespected. Think about what you might want to say in a situation like that. Starting with "I want you to" can be helpful here too. Practice saying it out loud. Here are some sample phrases to work with:

- "Don't talk to them like that!"
- "You need to ask before you touch."
- "That's disrespectful."
- "Please leave them alone."
- "It's not okay to talk to [or treat] people that way."

- "I don't find that funny."
- "That's not allowed here."
- "Take a step back."

Next time you're going to set a limit on your own behalf, remember how it felt to practice doing it for others and try to use some of that energy for yourself.

Laura's Story
"Give me your puppy"

Laura's a serious dog lover and a professional dog walker. She heard a news story about a dog stolen from its human at gunpoint. She was texting a friend about what happened and realized that her fierce protectiveness of dogs could help her stand up for herself. She texted:

Speaking of which, I'm going to self-defense class on Wednesday . . .

Hmm, maybe that's the key to self-defense. Bring the inner She-Hulk out by pretending they are trying to take my puppy. Provides much more courage and rage than just defending my inconsequential little self . . .

I'm now picturing all my practice role-play scenarios being "Give me your puppy" . . . "NO!!!!!!!!!!!!!!!!!!!"

Someone being shady making my Spidey Sense tingle? Assume they're about to say, "Give me your puppy." I'll be ready to kick some ass if they make a move.

To get more comfortable telling people what's okay with you and what's not, practice in lower-stress situations, like:

- Telling a friend that they can't have a bite of your food, can't use your phone, or can't borrow your clothes

- Telling someone that you can get back to them in two days

- Telling a roommate that you want them to wear headphones so you don't have to hear their music or games

- Telling someone that you won't give them a ride, help them with their homework, or watch their kids.

Move on to harder things, like telling someone you're not interested in another date or in hanging out after work, or that you can't make it to their destination wedding.

PART 3

If It Doesn't Work

If you've set a limit and repeated yourself as needed, and still someone's pushing your boundaries, it's time to switch strategies. What power or choices do you have when the other person isn't respecting your "no"?

You have the power of your own behavior. You have the choices you're able to make.

You might choose to stop seeing them. You might drop a class, ask to be taken off a project at work, ask to be assigned to a different workstation, or sign up for a different shift. You might have to literally change the locks on your doors. Block the person on your phone and on social media. Break up with them. Change jobs. Cut off their access to your children. Report them to management. Stop going to family events. Tell them you won't hang out with them when they're drunk—and do it. End the conversation every time they bring up the subject you told them you wouldn't discuss (your queerness, your vaccination status, your weight, your choice of partner, your haircut, their bigoted ideas about other people . . . you get the idea). Don't be there for it.

We're not saying these things are easy or simple. They're difficult, complicated, and loaded. They also may have unpleasant consequences for you—ranging from your friends gossiping about you to losing your job and more.

<u>NAME THE CONSEQUENCE.</u> Here are some examples of boundaries and their consequences. Practice saying these sentences out loud to make it easier when you have to set a boundary in real life. If you have a friend you can practice with, that's great! If not, be sure to say them out loud anyhow. When you're done with the examples below, write some of your own.

- "If you yell at me, I'll leave."

- "If you continue to criticize my [life choices, parenting, partner, weight, etc.], I won't hang out with you anymore."

- "Just a heads-up: I need to get off the phone in ten minutes." [Ten minutes later . . .] "I've got to go now!"

- "You're not respecting my limit, so I'm going to leave."

-

-

-

Sometimes it takes privilege to set a limit and deliver consequences if the harassment, abuse, or assault continues. To be able to leave a job or a partner. To be able to push back against someone who has more power.

But in virtually every situation, we have options. And options are where our power lies.

Here's how advice columnist (and boundary expert) Carolyn Hax put it in one live chat:

> *All of this grows out of the taproot of boundaries: that YOU decide what you think, what you discuss, whom you see, where you go, how you spend your time, what you value, where you live, how you guide the trajectory of your life. You. Other people can have opinions but that doesn't affect any of the preceding unless *you* decide to let it.*
>
> *Once you know this to be true in your very core, feel it, then it gets a lot easier to know when and how to tell people to back the erf [sic] off.*
>
> *And easier to withstand the blowback of people who are suddenly hitting a wall with you instead of pushing you around as usual. It's hard. (Understatement.)*

This isn't always easy. In fact, it never is. But you can do it.

Especially if someone's abusing or stalking you, you'll need to be conscious and cautious about how you make these changes. If that's your situation, please go to the Resources section to get support and guidance from an expert safety planner before taking any steps.

Lauren's Story
Going no-contact

My parents, especially my mother, had a hard time with me being a lesbian. My mother said awful things to me, refused to invite my partner to family events, and generally made it known that she wasn't okay with who I was.

After struggling with her for a few years, trying to convince her of my worthiness and my humanity, I took a break. I wrote my parents telling them that I wouldn't communicate via phone or in person with them for some time, and that their behavior would need to change before I would be in contact. I wrote a list of what they'd need to do differently, including recognizing my partner as my partner.

After almost a year, we worked things out. I got the break I needed and some clarity. They agreed to change their ways. I don't know if my mother's heart changed, but her behavior did, and that was all I needed.

PART 4

Asking for What You Want

If you DON'T ASK, the answer's always "NO."

Most of the assertiveness we've talked about so far has been about boundary setting: telling people what's okay and not okay with us. The other kind of assertiveness is asking for what we want.

It can mean telling a friend what you'd like to do this weekend, telling your partner you'd like an evening off from being with the kids, or asking for a shift change at work. It can mean checking in with someone about whether they want to be sexual with you.

It means not always putting our feelings, needs, and wants last. It means, as we discussed earlier, believing we deserve to be treated well and that our feelings, needs, and wants matter.

It also means fully understanding the fact that no one can read our minds, and no one will magically know what we need and give it to us (despite what some books and movies tell us).

If you want your roommate to stop leaving dishes in the sink, your partner to buy you flowers on your birthday, your boss to promote you, or your lover to press harder or softer during sex or a massage, you're going to have to tell them.

Being direct with what you want and need not only increases the chances you'll get it, it's also respectful of the other person. Hinting isn't the way to go.

All the other principles of assertiveness also apply to asking for what you want.

I WANT YOU TO. Think about your bottom lines in a relationship. It could be a romantic or sexual relationship or it could be another important relationship, like with a parent, child, or roommate.

Some bottom lines are pretty basic and widely shared, like "No hitting."

Others might be more specific to you, your emotional needs, and your history, like "When I get home, I want you to greet me at the door" or "Don't tell me I'm 'cute'; if you want to compliment me, please say I'm 'beautiful/handsome.'"

Pick one of your bottom lines and create a sentence with it, like one of the ones above.

Make sure your request is specific and measurable. If you say something like "I want you to respect me," the other person won't know what behaviors to change, and neither of you will be able to point to something and say it's happening—or it's not.

Instead, in the case of the respect example, ask for the things that would signify respect. Maybe you want them to show up on time when they say they will or listen to you without interrupting.

Now say your "I want you to . . ." sentence to a trusted friend. (You can also write the dialogue or record it on your phone.) If you're with a person, have them nod and say, "Okay."

Do this a few times. You can try different requests or different phrasings of the same request. The goal is to get more comfortable asking for what you want and to notice any feelings it brings up.

––––––––––

Because society is in many ways anti-sexual and prudish, few of us have learned to communicate directly about sex and desire. Sexual assertiveness means knowing yourself and your needs, desires, and limits, being able to advocate for what you want, and embracing your right to pleasure. It's important to be able to talk about what does and doesn't feel good to you, physically and emotionally. It's also important to be able to understand your (potential) partner's desires and limits.

WHAT I LIKE. With a trusted friend or lover, take turns asking and answering these questions; you can also write or draw the answers here or in a notebook, or you can record them on your phone.

- What's a kind of touch you like? What's a kind of touch you dislike? How do you know if you like or don't like a kind of touch?

- If someone's doing a kind of touch you like, how do you let them know?

- If someone's doing a kind of touch you dislike, how do you let them know?

- What's something you'd like to say to a (potential) sex partner about touch that you want or don't want?

DO YOU WANT TO . . . ? Imagine you're with someone and you think they want to be sexual, but you're not sure. Write the words you could use to clarify what they want, assuming you *aren't* interested in sex with them, either at this moment or ever. You can get across your message kindly and respectfully.

_____

_____

_____

_____

Next, write the words you could use to clarify what they want, and let them know that you *are* interested in sex with them, either at this moment or later. Then write some words you could use when *you* want to initiate sex.

_____

_____

_____

_____

SKILLS TO WORK ON. Take another look at this list of assertiveness basics.

- Take up space with your voice, body, and face.
- Tell the other person what you want them to do.
- Be direct: avoid excuses, explanations, and apologies.
- Name the behavior.
- Stay on your own agenda.
- Repeat yourself and get more intense.

Below, note the skills that are your priorities to work on and any steps you'll take.

- _____

- _____

- _____

WHAT CAN I SAY NEXT TIME? Go back to your story from Chapter 2. Now that you know more, you have the chance to think about what you'd say if a similar situation came up in the future. With your coach as a guide, imagine yourself taking an active, assertive role. Write what you could say using assertiveness skills and principles. Practice saying it out loud. If possible, say it to a trusted friend or family member. If that's not for you, say it to a video of a YouTuber, TikTok-er, or TV newsperson. It's harder than talking when no one's there, but less hard than talking to a live human. Revise the scene so you emerge safe and with your dignity. Keep at it even if doubts creep in. Have your coach reinforce you. In this way, you fortify your ability to resist.

_____

_____

_____

_____

FAN THE FLAMES 8. Think about a time—or times—when you've done one or more of the things on the assertiveness list, like telling someone what you want them to do, using a lead-in line, or skipping saying an unnecessary "sorry." Write down these successes. Even if you haven't done any of these things, write down any times you've noticed the possibility of doing them.

_____

_____

_____

_____

_____

_____

TIME FOR PRACTICE. Given everything you know now about setting a limit and asking for what you want, write in the bubbles what you could say in each of the situations below. This gets easier with practice—the more you do it, the more easily the sentences will come. (Before you read these situations, please take a few deep breaths and perhaps do some other type of self-care.)

Marita met Mateo at a party. She liked him and gave him her number. The next day, without asking, he sent a dick pic.

DJ was really looking forward to a low-key weekend after an exhausting week. On Friday, a friend called and said, "One of my other friends bailed and I really need you to help me move tomorrow. It'll probably only take about four hours, and I'll buy you pizza."

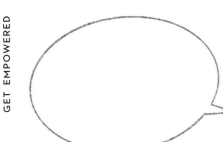

Dakota's best friend's partner showed up at Dakota's door. The partner seemed upset—and drunk. They asked to come in and talk. Dakota was alone and didn't want to let them in.

Aarti was meeting with her boss. She noticed after a while that the boss wasn't listening and was staring at her breasts.

Saara joined her parents and their new neighbors in the hot tub. One of the neighbors kept trying to give her a foot massage and made comments about her body that no one else could hear because the jets were loud. She moved away, but the neighbor followed and kept touching her.

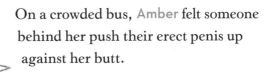

On a crowded bus, Amber felt someone behind her push their erect penis up against her butt.

Charlie was sitting on the bleachers with his friends at a game. Someone sat down and started chatting. They asked to borrow Charlie's friend's phone to share their number. When they reached for the phone, their hand grazed Charlie's groin. Charlie thinks it wasn't an accident.

While Kim and her father were talking about church, her father said, "I have nothing against homosexuals, but they shouldn't be allowed to participate in services."

Michelle was walking down the street with her white mobility cane. Without warning, someone grabbed her arm and started steering her along.

Ash was waiting in line. The person behind them said loudly, "What are you? A girl or a guy? I can't tell."

Practicing will make it easier to be assertive and will lead to deeper changes. As you work on assertiveness, be patient. Perhaps at first you'll only notice what you might have said and will be disappointed at what you didn't do or say. Try not to focus on the disappointment. Instead, see that noticing you might have done something is a step in the right direction. Focusing on the positive helps us get where we want to be. So keep focusing on what you *are* doing and where you want to go.

Remember, you can be assertive and still be harassed, abused, or assaulted. You also have a right to *not* be assertive. There's no one correct way to keep yourself safer. You can make a bunch of decisions you feel are unwise, and you still don't deserve to have your boundaries crossed. We can't control aggressors, and their actions are their responsibility.

De-escalation
Another way to stay safe

Most of the time, assertiveness is a practical way to protect yourself. But in some high-stakes situations, such as when a partner is being abusive, when someone's threatening to out you, or when the attacker has a weapon, de-escalation may be safer and more effective.

De-escalation is a way to reduce the possibility of violence. The goal is to calm the other person so you can get to safety.

When you're de-escalating, you don't need to agree or feel aligned in your heart with what you're doing. For example, you may apologize for something you don't feel sorry about or you're not responsible for. De-escalation is simply a *strategy* for increasing your safety.

When you decide to de-escalate, follow these five steps.

1. Anchor yourself: Breathe deeply and visualize your goal (for example, "I want to be able to leave" or "I want them to step back").

2. Assess for safety: Where is the safest place for you to be? If possible, stand or sit where each one of you could leave without having to go "through" the other one. Who else is around? If there are others, could they be helpful to you? Might they be threats?

3. Show your cool: Be calm in your facial expression and body language. Stand at a forty-five-degree angle diagonal to them with your hands visible. That allows them to see and feel that they have an escape.

4. Ask, listen, and empathize: These are the core of de-escalation, and can sound like:

    - "I'm sorry that happened."

    - "Tell me about the problem."

    - "That sounds really upsetting."

    - "How can I help?"

    - "I'd be furious too."

5. Find a safe exit: Ask or tell them to leave, or leave yourself if it's safe to do so. Give them an out. For example, you could say, "Listen, leave right now and I won't tell anyone about what happened." (Whether or not you then tell is totally up to you.)

Some other de-escalation strategies you might find helpful are:

- Agree (even if you don't really) or take their side.

- Solve the problem (if you can). If you can make yourself safer by doing what the person wants (for example, handing over your wallet or remaking their burrito), that's a smart choice. Or show the person that you'll take action. For example, hand them a piece of paper and a pen and say, "Please write down all your concerns and I'll make sure the manager sees it."

- Delay the interaction. Plan to continue when someone else can join you or when people are calmer. In a sexual assault, think of it as better time, better place. You can say: "Why do this here? Let's go to my place where it's more comfortable . . ." This is a version of going along that may give you opportunities to escape or resist.

- Create a distraction. Distracting someone also can buy you time or create an opening for escape or resistance.

Some things to avoid, as tempting as they may be: Don't point at them, and don't touch them. Don't call them names or use put-downs. Don't invade their space. Don't tell them to be quiet (instead, you can match their volume and then bring it down slowly). Be as respectful of them as you want them to be of you.

De-escalation isn't the same as losing. In fact, you can think of it as making the choice to "lose to win" (sometimes temporarily), and in some situations, it can be the best way to support your survival, safety, and well-being.

For more on de-escalation and negotiation, go to getempoweredbook.com.

Am I a Bad Person?

People raised as girls often feel like a "bad person" when they start to say "no." We don't even know you and we can honestly say this: YOU ARE NOT A BAD PERSON!

If you feel unable to speak up because you feel like you don't matter, notice that. What are the sentences that come into your brain when you start to speak up for yourself? Where's the feeling in your body that shuts you down? These feelings are real, but the rules are wrong.

You're not a bad person if you don't want to do everything that's asked of you. You're not a bad person if you stop the people-pleasing. You're not a bad person if you set limits. You're not a bad person if you ask for what you want.

We all deserve to be whole human beings with our own feelings, needs, and wants. To be able to speak our feelings, needs, and wants out loud might feel like we're violating some rules—because we are. Let's break the rules that say we don't matter or that we're not as important as others.

Society trains most of us to be compliant and passive and to put ourselves last. Changing that is hard work, so please be patient with yourself and celebrate your small successes! Fan the flames!

TL;DR

- Assertiveness is saying what you feel, need, or want directly. It's different from being passive (letting people walk all over you) or aggressive (disrespecting someone's boundaries and humanity).

- The basic elements of assertiveness are: taking up space with your voice, body, and face; telling them what you want them to do; being direct: avoiding excuses, explanations, and apologies; naming their behavior; staying on your own agenda; and repeating yourself and getting more intense.

- "I" statements are a helpful tool for stating what you feel, need, and want, where you take responsibility for your own feelings and don't accuse the other person.

- You can also use lead-in lines, go back later, or imagine you're protecting someone else to bolster your assertiveness.

- If you've set a limit and repeated yourself as needed, and still someone's pushing on your boundaries, it's time to engage your power in other ways.

- You can protect yourself and create the life you want not only by saying what's okay with you and what's not, but also by asking for what you want.

- In particular, people raised as girls often feel like a "bad person" when they start to say "no." We don't even know you and we can honestly say this: YOU ARE NOT A BAD PERSON!

THE HEART OF THE MATTER. *What's the best thing (okay, maybe three best things, since there was a lot here) you're going to remember from this chapter? Did you have an aha moment? Did you gain a skill—or four? Do you better understand what assertiveness is and how to make it happen? You don't have to answer these exact questions, but please do note your takeaways.*

SELF-CARE BREAK. *Take a deep breath. What self-care will you do now that you've finished this chapter? It can be a small thing (like a few seconds of stretching) or something bigger (like a day off). For more ideas, check in with the plan you made on page xix or the ideas we list on page 10.*

YOU'VE COME SO FAR! *There's loss in letting go of old ways of being and doing. But a safer, more authentic life is totally worth it.*

"RARELY, IF EVER, ARE ANY OF US HEALED IN ISOLATION. HEALING IS AN ACT OF COMMUNION."

—bell hooks

Chapter 10

WHAT'S NEXT

Get Support, Build Your Crew, Change the World

GROUNDING & CENTERING: Seek and find. Pause. Take a breath. Center yourself in your body. Take in your surroundings and name five things you can see, four things you can touch, three things you can hear, two things you can smell, and one thing you can taste. Any practice like this can help ground you if you're stressing or having a flashback by drawing your attention to your environment and your sensations in the present moment.

Harassment, abuse, and assault are traumatic to the mind, body, and spirit. They don't end with the event; the damage they cause can continue. If someone hurts you, the first thing to do is to make sure you're in a safe place. Then, the priority is healing. In this chapter, we'll talk more about how to get support, how to build your crew for longer-term care and community, and how to put some energy into ending gender-based violence.

All the suggestions here can be helpful whether or not you've directly experienced harassment, abuse, or assault, and whether or not you identify as a survivor. We all have been harmed by living in a world where gender-based violence is so widespread.

PART 1

Get Support

ASK FOR HELP

We all need support in dealing with the harassment, abuse, or assault that's happened—or is happening—to us. If someone's crossed your boundaries, whether in a big way or a small one, part of claiming your power and transforming your life is healing. You may need psychological, physical, emotional, spiritual, or financial support. You may need several—or all—of them. (You'll find counseling, support groups, and safety-planning help in the Resources section starting on page 245.)

For many, reaching out to supportive friends, family, or others who hold you up in everyday life makes the most sense. Research backs this up. In one experiment, people stood at the bottom of a hill and estimated its steepness. Those who had a friend with them estimated it to be less steep than those who assessed the hill when they were alone. Even people who *imagined* a friend with them thought the hill was less steep than those who didn't. Connection is powerful.

But if your friends, family, or others you talk to aren't helpful, you'll have to keep looking until you find people who believe you and in your right to be safe.

One reason you may need to keep looking is that those close to you often have their own feelings about what was done to you. They might tell you what to do or judge your behavior in an effort to manage their emotions. Keep talking to people until you find someone who'll give you the support you want, need, and deserve.

And getting help and info from people who are experts in aiding those who've experienced gender-based violence can make a difference that even the most supportive friends and family can't.

Asking for help can be hard in general because U.S. culture values independence and self-reliance so much. The shame and blame directed at survivors of gender-based violence make it harder. And interpersonal violence disrupts human connection, making it even more difficult to reach out. But human connection is also where most healing happens, so we encourage you to take the risk.

Of course, you don't <u>have</u> to tell anyone you don't want to tell. Telling is to help <u>you</u>, and you get to be in charge. If you decide to tell someone, you also get to decide how much detail you share. You don't have to answer their questions, and you don't have to take care of their feelings about it. Telling is for <u>you</u>.

One way you can improve the chances of getting what you need is to tell people how you want them to support you. You can let them know what responses you want or don't want. For example:

- "I'm going to tell you something, and I want you to listen and support me. Please don't make suggestions or try to fix my problem."

- "You know what happened to me. Would you sit with me while I text a hotline?"

- "Hearing you criticize the decisions I made about [my relationship/ what I did that day/what I was wearing/how I respond to street harassment/etc.] is painful. Could you just listen instead?"

- "So that's what I wanted to tell you. Would you tell me you still care about me and support me?"

If those you reach out to don't, won't, or can't support you in the way you want or need, try not to take it personally (we know that's not easy). It's not about you; it's about their limitations. Often their reaction comes from their own experiences, from their fear (and a need to believe it won't happen to them), or from their powerlessness (maybe about not being able to protect you). In any of these situations, they're centering themselves and their own needs rather than focusing on you.

Groups and institutions can compound the harm if you tell them what happened and they don't support you. Schools, religious groups, workplaces, and the criminal legal system are among the worst culprits.

Hold on to your knowledge that what was done to you was wrong and that you didn't deserve it. It can be disappointing, heartbreaking, and enraging if others don't understand that. But there's no one right way to respond to violations, and no one has the right to judge what you did or didn't do.

REMEMBER: the aggressors are responsible.

Many of us don't have anyone we can talk to who'll believe us or be supportive. Particularly if a partner or other family member has abused you, you may have been isolated from important people in your life and other support networks, making it harder to know who to ask for help.

While that's awful, it doesn't mean you have to give up. You can keep asking, or you can reach out to the groups in the Resources section on page 245. The important thing is that you make the connection.

WHO CAN I TELL? Think about who in your life you feel would be most likely to listen to you and be responsive when you tell them what you need. Write any names here. (You can always reach out to the groups in the Resources section instead of or in addition to anyone in your own life.)

_____

_____

_____

_____

_____

_____

<u>WHAT'S IN THE WAY.</u> If you have barriers to asking for support, name them now. All kinds of things could get in your way, like: "They might tell me it's no big deal," "They may not believe me," or "The shelter might not accept me because of my gender." Write them here.

How would you feel if that happened? What would you do next? If you named barriers, write or draw an encouragement for yourself too.

<u>MY FIRST-AID KIT.</u> Imagine you reach out for support and you don't get it. What might you need if that happens? Write down what self-care you'll do if you don't get the help you're looking for. Affirmations like "I deserve support" can also be helpful.

Finally, write down who else you'll reach out to if you don't get what you need the first time.

SPEAK YOUR TRUTH

Part of healing from harassment, abuse, or assault may be claiming your voice and breaking your silence. Speaking up about what happened to you is a huge deal—and it's not a one-time thing.

Some strategies you can try as part of your healing include:

- If a partner or other family member abused you, work with an advocate or counselor to make a plan to keep yourself as safe as possible while you're still in contact with them or after you leave. (See the Resources section, especially the National Sexual Assault Hotline and the National Domestic Violence Hotline, for ways to find an advocate or counselor who's been trained in trauma and gender-based violence.)

- Learn about common reactions to abuse and assault and what the healing process has been like for others (see many of the groups in the Resources section).

- If you can, break the silence by putting the responsibility on the aggressor, warning others, or sharing information as a way to regain your power. (Unfortunately, breaking the silence can sometimes open you to backlash, so if you decide to do it, have a plan for how you'll keep yourself safe and get support.)

- Make decisions about what other actions you might want to take to try to hold the aggressor accountable.

If you can do it safely, it *may* be empowering to confront the person who mistreated you. Only you'll know if that's right for you. If you decide to, here are some ways to do it:

- Write to the aggressor (see the next exercise for more on that).

- Tell a group the aggressor's affiliated with (like a professional organization, union, faith group, or business) what they did.

- Speak directly to the aggressor. You can pick the time and place, which can rebalance the power. Whether it's in person, on the phone, via text or email, on Zoom or FaceTime, or some other way, you might ask someone to be with you while you do it.

You can speak up at any time; unless you plan to take legal action (which has deadlines), you can be flexible about when and if you do.

HAVING MY SAY. Write or record your message to the person who harmed you. You don't have to send the letter, email, text, or video; it can be empowering to create it whether you do or not. In whatever you write or say:

- Describe their problematic behavior.
- Include how you felt about it at the time and how you feel about it now.
- Include what you'd like them to do to repair the harm they caused.

You can decide later whether to send it. If you do send it, keep in mind that you can't control the aggressor's reaction. You're sending the letter because you want to have your say, not because you expect them to change or understand (although that would be lovely).

Here's how Nadia followed up after being assaulted in the thrift store.

Nadia's Story
Back to the thrift store

A while after my experience at the thrift store, I summoned the courage to tell my women's support group what had happened. They helped me get in touch with my anger about it, and I was relieved to hear similar stories from others. A few women decided to go to the store with me to demand that this employee get fired.

The boss refused to fire the employee, so we threatened a picket line. Eventually, he was let go. Ah, the power of solidarity!

PART 2

Build Your Crew

Connection is essential to healing from gender-based violence. Harassment, abuse, and assault rupture our relationships with other humans. This is especially true if the aggressor is someone we know, and even more so if they're someone we trusted, loved, or relied on. When people cross our boundaries and harm us, it's a betrayal of an essential human pact.

The guilt, self-blame, and shame that society imposes on us exacerbate the harm.

The fact that we in the U.S. live in a society and culture that emphasizes the individual over the family, group, and community—and that values independence so much—also makes it harder for survivors to get what we need to heal.

But we can repair some of the harm by connecting with others, especially other survivors.

So in addition to asking for help, we encourage you to put some energy toward finding people who can be there for you beyond the immediate healing process. They can be in person or online. They don't even have to be people you talk with about your experience with harassment, abuse, and assault; it's simply important to have connections to other humans, even if you're an introvert.

FIND MY PEOPLE. Below is a list of places you may find folks you enjoy spending your time with (virtually or in person). You can use this list in two ways.

1. Circle or check people or groups you are already connected with and add any others you have that aren't listed.

2. Highlight those you'd consider reaching out to, joining, or adding to your life.

☐ Support groups, whether a survivor group or another group based on shared identity or experience, like a health condition, caregiving, or a twelve-step program

☐ Craft or other creative group

☐ Dance, yoga, martial arts, hiking, or running group or class. People you work out with. Any kind of movement is especially good for moving trauma out of the body.

☐ Sports teams (same as above on the positive effects of movement). Even informal ones like shuffleboard meetups or volleyball pickup games.

☐ Drumming circle, chorus, band—any kind of music-making

☐ Faith group, meditation group

☐ Community garden group

☐ Karaoke or trivia friends

☐ Book club, writing group, gaming friends

☐ Work colleagues or professional network, employee resource group, or union

☐ Parent group, parent-teacher organization, parenting friends, your kids' friends' parents

☐ Neighborhood group

☐ Study group, campus organization

☐ Military family group

☐ Dog-walking pals

☐ People you volunteer with

☐

☐

☐

☐

☐

☐

☐

PART 3

Change the World

Getting involved in ending harassment, abuse, and assault is a powerful way to continue your own healing while supporting others, preventing harm, and ultimately, changing the world.

So many of us who do work to end sexist and racist violence are survivors, and we value both the individual and the collective reasons to do this work.

Taking action can also create connection and community with others who share your commitment and who are acting together in a shared cause.

There are as many ways to get involved as there are humans. If you want to make a difference, consider what approach might be best for you.

> [PRACTICING RADICAL SELF-CARE] MEANS WE'RE ABLE TO BRING OUR ENTIRE SELVES INTO THE MOVEMENT. IT MEANS THAT WE INCORPORATE INTO OUR WORK AS ACTIVISTS WAYS OF ACKNOWLEDGING AND HOPEFULLY ALSO MOVING BEYOND TRAUMA. IT MEANS A HOLISTIC APPROACH.
>
> —*Angela Davis*

Because every type of oppression is expressed and reinforced through violence, you can choose to work on creating a safer, more respectful world where people can be themselves by working on ending sexism, racism, heterosexism, cis sexism, fat hatred, ableism, xenophobia, classism, or religious and cultural persecution (such as hatred of Sikhs, Muslims, or Jews).

Because all these issues are related, and because everyone has multiple identities, it's important to include all the people and systems affected in whatever you're doing.

You can take action in ways small and big, from disagreeing with someone when they make a biased comment to making social and economic justice your life's work. What you do and how you do it is totally up to you. Let what calls to you and what works for your life guide you in deciding how you want to act.

Here are some ideas; keep in mind that, depending on identity and experience, not all of these will be good choices for everyone.

1. SUPPORT SURVIVORS AND THOSE WHO DEFEND THEMSELVES

- Support people in setting boundaries and taking care of themselves. Give positive feedback to women, queer people, BIPOC, and members of other oppressed groups who set limits.

- Volunteer at a hotline, shelter, sexual assault agency, or similar program.

- Confront harassers, abusers, and attackers when it's safe to do so.

- Advocate for those who are criminalized for fighting back.

- Learn to recognize signs of abuse and what to do if you think a friend, neighbor, family member, or coworker is being abused.

- Support someone who's being harassed in your workplace or at school.

- Take a workshop to learn active-bystander skills.

2. STOP VIOLENCE WITH THOSE CLOSE TO YOU

- Promote healthy attitudes about sexuality.

- Practice respect at home.

- Work on your own sexism, racism, ableism, and other biases.

- Teach children to treat others with respect, and that they also deserve to be treated with respect. Educate them from the time they're little about consent in everyday life, including that it's okay to say "no" to adults.

- Teach children healthy ways to express feelings and manage conflict.

- Become someone who others will tell if they're harassed, attacked, or abused, and know how to respond. (See "What to Say—and What Not to Say—When Someone Tells You They Have Been Sexually Assaulted" by Lauren R. Taylor under "Books and Articles We Love" in the Resources.)

- Develop a comprehensive policy against harassment at your school, workplace, faith group, etc.

- When people make oppressive comments about women, LGBTQIA+ people, Jews, BIPOC, immigrants, disabled people, or religious minorities, tell them why those comments aren't okay. Do the same when you hear anyone shaming or blaming survivors.

- Talk to people about sexism and rape acceptance in music, movies, and other forms of culture. Pay closer attention to misogynistic themes in media, including movies that romanticize stalking.

3. SPREAD THE WORD ABOUT EMPOWERMENT SELF-DEFENSE

- Advocate for the right to defend yourself, especially for BIPOC and LGBTQIA+ people, who are most likely to be criminally punished for defending themselves.

- Tell people about empowerment self-defense classes. Become an empowerment self-defense teacher.

- Let people know that empowerment self-defense is for people of all ages and abilities.

4. ADDRESS VIOLENCE ON A STRUCTURAL LEVEL

- Write to news editors, to politicians, and to companies, objecting to sexist, heterosexist, racist, or other oppressive views and actions.

Comment on social media posts, especially ones where companies or people in power will see them.

- If you have a blog, a podcast, a TikTok account, a YouTube channel, or any other platform, use it to speak out about gender-based violence and other forms of oppression.

- Give money to or get involved with organizations fighting racism, sexism, heterosexism, and other oppressions, including programs promoting healthy masculinity.

- Don't buy from companies that use racist or sexist images. Object to their advertising, gaming content, and other oppressive materials.

- Ask organizations you're active in (like your church or neighborhood group) to take public stances on racism, sexism, and violence.

- Join, donate to, volunteer for, or raise money for anti-violence organizations.

- Work to develop ways to hold accountable those who harass, abuse, and attack that don't involve the criminal legal system and locking people up. Learn about and advocate for alternative approaches to addressing interpersonal violence, such as restorative and transformative justice.

- Work for legal and cultural changes that prevent harassment, abuse, and assault, and that support survivors.

- Show up to protests if you can, or support the organizers behind the scenes.

- Get politically active locally, nationally, or internationally.

- Support gun-control laws.

- Support candidates who take constructive positions on racism, sexism, and heterosexism and who understand violence and oppression. Vote.

5. WORK TO INCREASE THE POWER OF PEOPLE IN MARGINALIZED GROUPS

- Support efforts to decriminalize sex work.

- Work to increase the security and standard of living for those in marginalized groups, including addressing poverty, housing, wages, health insurance, and childcare. Get active in your local mutual aid group.

- Get involved in your community to support those most marginalized and thus most likely to experience violence.

- Make visible the often-ignored violence against Indigenous women, sex workers, bisexuals, people with physical and developmental disabilities, and trans people.

While you're doing all this good work, be sure to make time for fun, inspiration, joy, and celebration!

MY TURN. Ask yourself if you have the bandwidth to add some kind of activism—big or small—to your life. Some, like speaking up when you hear a racist or sexist remark, can take courage and mental and emotional energy but won't require a time commitment. Others require carving out space in your life. Keep this in mind as you decide what you want to do, if anything.

If the answer's yes, you do have the bandwidth and look forward to the rewards of taking action, write your own ideas to add to the list. Then put a check next to one to three actions you'd like to take.

_____

_____

_____

_____

While changing the world is often very fulfilling, be sure to nurture and feed yourself while doing it. Continue to ask for what you need, and step back and take care of yourself.

Change is a long, and often painful, process. Not only have we all been learning—filling in the gaps in our skills, growing into our true selves—but the world has been changing too. And that's because people in oppressed groups have made it happen.

When Nadia and Lauren first started working on gender-based violence, this was the landscape:

- There was no recognition of, and no word for, workplace sexual harassment or street harassment.
- People had only recently started sexual assault centers, and shelters for abused women didn't exist.
- Acquaintance, spousal, and partner rape weren't legally or socially recognized.

Those are just a few examples.

Although much more work needs to be done, it's important to celebrate the progress we've made. People are finally recognizing how common interpersonal violence is, thanks in large part to the MeToo movement, which has broken so much silence around and empowered so many survivors. Lady Gaga, Lizzo, Rihanna, Taylor Swift, and others have made speaking up part of their platform and their music. Some criminalized survivors, like Marissa Alexander, Ky Peterson, and Bresha Meadows, have been freed. There are men who deeply understand gender-based violence, who are addressing it, and who are working with other men about the problem and their role in solving it.

It's a good start. Now it's up to all of us to continue building a world of equity, respect, and safety for everyone.

TL;DR

- We all need support to deal with the harassment, abuse, and assault we've experienced, even if they're only "small," annoying interactions. We help you brainstorm places to find support and connection, including family and friends, and professionals like hotlines, counselors, and support groups.

- People often don't know how to show up for survivors, so you may need to fortify yourself to keep asking until you get what you need.

- Connection is essential to healing, so beyond the immediate healing process, building your networks can be transformative.

- Breaking the silence about what you've experienced can be healing, as long as you decide that doing so is best for you.

- Getting involved in ending harassment, abuse, and assault is a powerful way to continue your own healing while supporting others, preventing harm, and ultimately, changing the world.

THE HEART OF THE MATTER. *Did you have any aha moments while doing this chapter? Did you think of someone to reach out to, a new group to join, or a way to change the world? What's your "best thing" from this chapter? You can do whatever works for you: write it, draw or doodle it, tell a friend, or record it on your phone.*

SELF-CARE BREAK. *Take a deep breath. What self-care will you do now that you've finished this chapter? It can be a small thing (like a few seconds of stretching) or something bigger (like a day off). For more ideas, check in with the plan you made on page xix or the ideas we list on page 10.*

YOU'VE GOT CHOICES! *With support and some plans for action, you now have a lot more choices. And choices equal empowerment. Celebrate how far you've come!*

Chapter 11

CONCLUSION

Embrace Your Yes

GROUNDING & CENTERING: In my mind's eye. Have a friend read this to you or record it on your phone and play it back. (This visualization focuses on the beach, but if you're more of a woods or a desert person, or if you like another outdoor setting, you can revise it to work for you.)

You open a door and find yourself on a beach. While in the doorway, you see the sun is shining and glinting off the water, and the breeze moves gently against your face. The temperature is perfect. You move outside, feel the soft, warm sand underneath you. At the water's edge, the waves crash along the shore. Your toes get soaked with salt water. It feels cool and refreshing. Stay as long as you want, and when you're ready, go back inside.

Congratulations on completing this book! You've been brave, challenged yourself, and grown. To do this work, you had to be courageous, resilient, vulnerable, patient, and committed. You did that; celebrate it.

EVERY "NO" IS A "YES" TO SOMETHING ELSE.

Doing this work is a gift to yourself. It's saying you value yourself enough to stretch, let go of what doesn't serve you, go into some unknowns. Your life's probably more authentic, your relationship with yourself better. This opens the possibility of closer, more meaningful relationships with others too.

If you're focusing on mistakes you made or progress you still want to make, please offer yourself some compassion. Give yourself some love for what you *have* done, the progress you *have* made, the work you've done that matters even if you don't see progress. It's a process.

Just a few more things before you go . . .

PART 1

What Do You Want to Say "Yes" To?

Even though setting boundaries is a central focus of this book—you might even title it *1,001 Ways to Say "No"*—we're not all about the "no." We do say "no" to things that intrude on us, disrespect us, threaten us.

But we also say "no" so that we can say "yes" to the lives we want and to being our most authentic selves. Every "no" is a "yes" to something else: yes to time for something you want to do (even if that's nothing), yes to who you want to be, yes to yourself.

So what's next for you? What will you do with your more empowered, more healed self? What do you want your life to look like?

MY VISION FOR THE FUTURE. Imagine that your life is big, that you take up space, that you ask for what you want, that you feel aligned with your true self. Imagine that you feel intimidated or afraid only when danger is in fact brewing. What would your life be like?

Look back at what you wrote or created when envisioning the life you want in Chapter 1. Think about what you'd do if the world was a safe place. Has anything changed since you made that list?

Now take a few minutes to envision where you want to go from here. What's next? What do you want your life to look like? What do you have in your life now that you want to keep and what would you like to add? Write, draw, collage, sing, or otherwise create intentions, a vision, or aspirations to guide you.

PART 2

Celebrate Yourself

Now's the time to celebrate yourself and your efforts! The fact that you worked with this book is an expression of your self-love and a result of your persistence. Maybe you've made big changes—or perhaps you're just beginning to recognize the seeds of transformation inside you.

<u>**FAN THE FLAMES 9.**</u> Honor your strengths: your insights, understanding, determination, skills—both the ones you came to this book with and the new ones as a result of working through it. Write a list, draw a picture in a sketchbook, or narrate a story about your strengths and resources. You can include things like your values, personality, beliefs, support network, and more.

_____

_____

_____

_____

_____

<u>**A CONVERSATION WITH MYSELF.**</u> What's changed because you worked with this book? How is your more empowered self different? How do you feel, move, talk, relate to yourself and others, see the world and your place in it? Be sure to include the little things—the times you noticed you might have another choice, the times you felt more sure in yourself—as well as any big shifts.

As you move beyond this book, continue to fan those flames.

Write, draw, or record three ways you'll continue this conversation with yourself and with those who support you in making changes in yourself and the world. Be specific, as that helps make the changes real. So, for example, instead of saying, "I'll work on my confidence," say, "I'll speak up when my coworker teases me about my disability."

Then, one more time, write an affirmation about the fact that you deserve to be safe and to be treated with respect.

_____

_____

_____

Remember: change takes time, and it doesn't go in a straight line. There's not a moment when you're done. Even though Nadia and Lauren have spent their whole adult lives doing this work, we continue to find these issues challenging, and we continue to learn and grow. Learning and change are continuous and lifelong.

Disappointments, setbacks, and things that feel like failure will happen. That's okay—it's how growth works.

Have PATIENCE with yourself. Have COMPASSION for who you've been and LOVE for who you're becoming. You DID this!

One last reminder: it's not your fault! No matter what you did or didn't do, or what you do or don't do in the future, if you're harassed, abused, or attacked, the responsibility lies entirely with the aggressor.

Okay, okay, just one *more* thing: today, choose to treat yourself like someone you love.

TL;DR

- You did it! Doing this work is a gift to yourself; please acknowledge it.

- What are your "yes"es? What do you want to say "yes" to, what do you want to include in your life, what will you do with your more empowered, healed self?

- Honor your strengths, both the ones you had before reading *Get Empowered* and any new ones. What's changed because you worked with this book? As you move beyond the book, continue to fan those flames.

- Think about how you'll continue this conversation with yourself and those who support you.

- Celebrate your growth and success. And grant yourself grace and compassion for where you still want to go.

THE HEART OF THE MATTER. *Write, draw, collage, or record the best or most important things you're going to take away from your work with* Get Empowered.

SELF-CARE BREAK. *Take a deep breath. What self-care will you do now that you've finished this book? It can be a small thing (like a few seconds of stretching) or something bigger (like a day off). For more ideas, check in with the plan you made on page xix or the ideas we list on page 10.*

ABOUT EMPOWERMENT SELF-DEFENSE

Get Empowered is based on decades of work by practitioners of empowerment self-defense (ESD). Nadia and Lauren have each taught ESD for more than thirty-five years, and this book is a result of their time with tens of thousands of students.

Here we're going to tell you more about what ESD is and summarize the research on its effectiveness.

If you'd like to take an ESD class, you can find an ESD practitioner near you—or one who teaches online—at getempoweredbook.com. Also on the site you can sign up to get bonus content, additional resources for working with the book, and more.

WHAT EMPOWERMENT SELF-DEFENSE IS—AND ISN'T

When most people think of self-defense, especially women's self-defense training, they think of martial arts. While martial arts are great for a lot of things (like improving fitness and focus), they're not practical or realistic for the kinds of harassment, abuse, and assault people experience today.

ESD teaches practical skills to those targeted for gender-based violence—primarily women and LGBTQIA+ people. These skills help people avoid, interrupt, respond to, and heal from interpersonal violence.

We teach those skills in the context of rape culture, addressing the physical, mental, emotional, spiritual, and sociocultural components of advocating for and protecting yourself and others.

ESD is grounded in an understanding of social inequality and social justice, and it addresses the whole spectrum of gender-based violence, from harassment to attack, from microaggressions to trafficking.

In short, ESD is anything we think or say or do that helps us feel safe, strong, and respected.

These are some of the core elements of an ESD program.

- We know that trauma survivors are in every room, and we teach with awareness of how trauma affects people.

- We reject victim-blaming, and we honor anything anyone has done or is doing to survive.

- We focus a lot on harassment, abuse, and assault by people we know, as that's most common.

- We use and model consent throughout the class, and every activity in an ESD classroom is optional.

- We don't use fear tactics, and we focus on students' strengths rather than weaknesses and build on them.

- We practice assertive communication skills that can be used to interrupt all levels of violations, and we don't just teach physical self-defense.

- We teach a toolbox of skills—physical, verbal, emotional—against a range of assaults ranging from irritating to life-threatening.

- Our classes are accessible and include physical techniques that are simple, quick to learn, and easy to remember, and that people of different ages, sizes, and abilities can do.

- We know that whatever someone decides to do in each situation, whatever action they do or don't take, they aren't at fault. The responsibility lies 100% with the aggressor.

- We don't tell anyone what they should or shouldn't do. We recognize that there are many ways to defend oneself, and we respect everyone's decision to get through or survive the best way they can.

AND IT WORKS

The most profound testimony about the transformative power of ESD training is what our students say. They tell us how life changing ESD training has been for them: they are more able to speak up for themselves; are less likely to blame themselves for harassment, abuse, and assault; are more confident and less fearful; know themselves better; trust themselves more; have healthier relationships; and are more able to create the lives they want.

Research backs this up. Several studies have found that people who have taken an ESD class are more likely to avoid sexual assault if they're targeted and less likely to be targeted to begin with.

Studies also show ESD training decreases sexual harassment, sexual coercion, and physical violence. For example, in the year following taking an ESD class:

- College women in the U.S. were 37% less likely to experience assault of any kind, and none of those who took the self-defense class reported a rape.

- College women in Canada who took the class were 46% less likely to be raped, and 63% less likely to experience attempted rape, than those who hadn't taken the class.

- Teen girls in Kenya who had taken the class were 63% less likely to experience sexual assault than those who hadn't taken the class.

- Participants in a U.S. community class (that was much more diverse than the college groups) were 52% less likely to be sexually assaulted in any way and 58% less likely to experience unwanted intercourse (rape or sexual coercion) than those who didn't take the class.

In the six months after an ESD program, Indigenous girls in South Dakota were 80% less likely to be sexually assaulted and 26% less likely to be sexually harassed than those who didn't participate in the program.

Research also shows that ESD programs increase assertiveness, confidence, and self-esteem and lower fear and anxiety. They also reduce self-blame and help people heal from sexual assault.

Although research on ESD is solid, more is needed. For example, most of it has been done with college students, who tend to be similar in age, race, education, and social class. Research is needed that includes more people who aren't students, are gender expansive, are BIPOC, and who have disabilities, among other identities.

And again: if you'd like to take an ESD class, you can find an ESD practitioner near you—or one who teaches online—plus bonus content and more resources for working with this book, at getempoweredbook.com.

GLOSSARY

ABLEISM is prejudice and discrimination against people with disabilities; valuing nondisabled people more.

BIPOC stands for Black, Indigenous, and people of color. Unlike the terms *people of color* or *POC*, it highlights the fact that the U.S. was founded on the enslavement of Black people and the genocide of Indigenous peoples. The term encompasses all marginalized racial and ethnic groups, including Black, Indigenous, Latine, and Asian/Pacific Islander people; people can have more than one of these identities.

CISGENDER describes anyone who identifies with the sex they were assigned at birth; someone who isn't transgender. Also called *cis*.

CONSENT is when everyone involved wants something and agrees that it's okay. For example, if you say, "Is it okay if I hug you?" and the other person says, "Sure!" then you've both consented to a hug, but that doesn't mean a kiss is okay. Either of you can also change your mind mid-hug or make a different decision about hugs in the future. Consent isn't only about physical or sexual contact; it applies to almost everything that involves more than one person, like what time they can text you, whether you can tag them in a photo, whether you want them to take off their shoes in your home, whether you're okay with them sharing information about you, and more.

A **DEADNAME** is the name a trans or non-binary person was given at birth and no longer uses. Also a verb, as in "Please stop deadnaming me."

EMPOWERMENT SELF-DEFENSE teaches practical skills to those targeted for gender-based violence—primarily women and LGBTQIA+ people. The combination of verbal and physical skills works for avoiding, interrupting, responding to, and healing from the effects of interpersonal violence. It's what Nadia and Lauren teach and is the basis of *Get Empowered.* (Find out more in About Empowerment Self-Defense on page 237.)

GASLIGHTING is manipulating someone psychologically to try to get them to question their own reality, memory, sanity, experience, or perceptions. Most often seen in relationships where one person is being abusive, it also can be used in other situations where power is being abused, for example, after a rape.

GENDER-BASED VIOLENCE is harm done based on actual or perceived gender, sex, sexual orientation, or gender expression. It's a manifestation and reinforcement of unequal power relationships among genders and sexual orientations. It most commonly shows up as sexual violence (including sexual harassment), partner abuse, stalking, and sex trafficking. (For more, see the spectrum in Chapter 2.)

GENDER SOCIALIZATION is the process of teaching people how to behave according to gender roles. For example, gender stereotypes encouraging girls to be passive (girls are praised for being "good" and "nice") and boys to be aggressive (infant boys are played with more roughly than infant girls) or saying that girls are good at people skills and boys are good at sports and math. Parents, schools, and the media are the most common ways we learn what roles we're supposed to fill.

INTERNALIZED OPPRESSION is when members of an oppressed group adopt the beliefs and stereotypes about their own group that come from the dominant group. For example, dark-skinned people who use skin-lightening products, women who slut-shame other women, and LGBQA+ people who try to change their sexual orientation are all acting from internalized oppression.

LGBTQIA+, TWO SPIRIT, AND NON-BINARY are gender identities and sexual orientations. *L, G,* and *B* stand for *lesbian, gay,* and *bisexual. T* stands for *transgender,* meaning someone doesn't identify as the sex they were assigned at birth. *Q* can stand for *queer,* which many people use as an umbrella term for LGBTQIA+, or as a way of saying they don't belong in any of the categories or that they aren't straight. *Q* can also stand for *questioning,* which means someone feels they may not be straight or cisgender but isn't sure how they identify. *I,* or *intersex,* refers to someone with one or more innate sex characteristics, including genitals, internal reproductive organs, and chromosomes, that fall outside traditional concepts of male or female bodies. *A* stands for *asexual,* meaning someone who doesn't experience sexual attraction at all or experiences it only under certain circumstances, for example, after forming a strong emotional connection. *Two spirit* refers to a person who identifies as having both a masculine and a feminine spirit, and is used by some Indigenous people to describe their sexual, gender, and/or spiritual identity. *Non-binary, genderqueer,* or *gender diverse* describes those who experience their gender as falling outside the binary gender categories of "male" and "female."

MARGINALIZED refers to people and groups who, based on some aspect of their identity, are oppressed, discriminated against, and excluded in the social, political, economic, educational, legal, and/or cultural realms.

MICROAGGRESSIONS are common verbal, behavioral, or environmental slights, whether intentional or unintentional, that communicate hostile, derogatory, or negative attitudes toward stigmatized or culturally marginalized groups. They are manifestations of the dominant group's power and entitlement and can be a result of ignorance or malice.

PATRIARCHY is a social system in which cisgender men hold primary power and predominate in roles of political leadership, moral authority, social privilege, and control of property. In patriarchal societies, men largely hold the power and women are largely excluded from it.

RACISM is individual and systemic bias or discrimination against Black, Indigenous, Latine, Asian, and other people of color based on the belief that White identity is the norm and that BIPOC are lesser, problematic, or abnormal.

RAPE CULTURE is a culture in which sexual violence is pervasive and treated as normal, and victims are blamed for the assaults against them. It's not just about sexual violence itself but about cultural norms and institutions that protect those who rape, shame victims, and demand that women be responsible for avoiding sexual violence. The norms include things like victim-blaming, slut-shaming, sexual objectification, trivializing rape, denying how widespread sexual violence is, and refusing to acknowledge the harm it causes.

A **TRIGGER** is anything that sets off a memory of a traumatic experience. It can be a noise, smell, temperature, other physical sensation, or visual image. When we're triggered, we're usually so filled up with feelings related to the old trauma that we're unable to focus on the present, and we can't think rationally or regulate our emotions like we usually can.

VICTIM-BLAMING is examining the victim's or survivor's behavior to explain why violence happened rather than looking at the harasser's, abuser's, or attacker's behavior. This may look like believing that violence happens because of what victims are wearing, how drunk they were, or because they didn't disclose that they're transgender.

XENOPHOBIA is fear, hatred, or mistreatment of people from other countries or cultures.

RESOURCES

Get Help, Learn More, and Get Involved

Many more resources are available on the Get Empowered website at getempoweredbook.com. Also on the site you can sign up to get bonus content, additional resources for working with the book, and more.

SUPPORT, COUNSELING, HOTLINES, AND INFORMATION

1 in 6. *Support and resources for male survivors of sexual abuse and assault.* 877-565-8860; 1in6.org

ACLU Know Your Rights. *Covers "know your rights" for everything from LGBTQIA+ high school students to dealing with TSA to sexual assault in detention to immigration to what to do if your rights are violated at a demonstration, and more.* aclu.org/know-your-rights

American Civil Liberties Union. *To report an incident of hate or police misconduct, go to the ACLU site and find the chapter nearest you.* aclu.org

Asian Mental Health Collective. *A therapist directory, education, support groups, and other resources for Asian, Pacific Islander, and South Asian American (APISAA) people seeking mental health services.* asianmhc.org

Break the Cycle. *Educational programs for teens and parents on healthy relationships, abusive relationships, and legal rights.* 888-988-TEEN; breakthecycle.org

Council on American-Islamic Relations. *Resources on knowing your rights while protesting, with law enforcement, while traveling, etc., as well as links to chapters around the country. You can report an incident and they may take legal action on your behalf.* cair.com

The Deaf Hotline. *24-7 support for D/deaf abuse survivors through email, chat, and more.* hotline@adwas.org; adwas.org/hotline/national

EFT Universe. *Information on Emotional Freedom Technique (EFT)/tapping, a holistic healing technique for addressing trauma, chronic pain, stress, anxiety, and more.* eftuniverse.com/community-resources

Forge. *Resources for trans and non-binary people on safe dating, workplace sexual harassment, healing from partner violence, and more.* forge-forward.org/resources /trans-communities-2

HeartMob. *Support for people experiencing online harassment.* iheartmob.org

Love Is Respect. *National teen dating abuse hotline. Help for you, a friend, or your teen if you're a parent.* 866-331-9474 / 866-331-8453 TTY; loveisrespect.org

The Loveland Foundation. *A therapy fund, education, and wellness resource for Black women and girls.* thelovelandfoundation.org

Melanin and Mental Health. *A directory of therapists, educational resources, and wellness events, as well as a podcast for the BIPOC communities.* melaninandmentalhealth.com

me too. Movement. *Wide-ranging resources for survivors and those who care about them, including a resource library.* metoomvmt.org

National Abortion Hotline. *Information, referrals, financial assistance, and more in many languages for those seeking abortion care.* 800-772-9100; prochoice.org/patients /naf-hotline

National Coalition of Anti-Violence Programs. *An English and Spanish hotline, legal services, support groups, counseling, and advocacy and accompaniment for LGBTQIA+ people and people living with HIV who have survived any form of violence. Also provides a place to report hate crimes and other violence.* 212-714-1141; avp.org/ncavp

National Domestic Violence Hotline. *A 24-7 hotline for survivors of abuse offering free, confidential support, education, and referrals in more than two hundred languages. Provides personalized safety planning that includes ways to stay as safe as possible while in a relationship, leaving a relationship, and after you've left.* 800-799-7233; thehotline.org

National Human Trafficking Hotline. *Support, resources, referrals, and more for those being trafficked and those who want to help them.* 888-373-7888 / TTY 711; humantraffickinghotline.org

National Queer and Trans Therapists of Color Network. *A directory of therapists and educational resources and a therapy fund for QTBIPOC folks seeking mental health services.* nqttcn.com/en

National Sexual Assault Hotline. *Support, information, advice, resources, and referrals for those who've survived sexual violence and those who support them.* 800-656-HOPE (4673); rainn.org

National Street Harassment Hotline. *A 24-7 hotline in English and Spanish supporting those who've been sexually harassed in public spaces.* 855-897-5910; stopstreetharassment.org/our-work/nationalshhotline

The Network/La Red. *Survivor-led organizing to end partner abuse among lesbian, gay, bisexual, queer and/or transgender (LGBTQIA+) folks, as well as folks in kink and polyamorous communities. Offers a hotline in English and Spanish, support groups, and more.* 800-832-1901; tnlr.org

Open Path Psychotherapy Collective. *A directory of sliding-scale and low-cost therapists in the U.S.* openpathcollective.org

Our Bodies, Ourselves Today. *Information, resources, and referrals on all things health and sexuality, including birth control, menstruation, pregnancy and childbirth, and gender-based violence. (A total remake of the twentieth-century book.)* ourbodiesourselves.org

The Resilient Brain Project. *A list of free mental health resources, including apps, games, playlists, videos, articles, and more on subjects like stress, anxiety, depression, trauma, relationships, discrimination, and allyship.* resilientbrainproject.com

Resources and Support for Transgender Survivors (National Sexual Violence Resource Center). *Crisis lifelines, wellness resources, and programs for transgender survivors.* nsvrc.org/blogs/resources-and-support-transgender-survivors

Scarleteen. *Articles, live chat, and message boards with inclusive, comprehensive sex and relationship info for teens and young adults.* scarleteen.com

Sex Workers Outreach Project USA (SWOP-USA). *General support, advice, crisis counseling, referrals, and information about safety and legal rights.* 877-776-2004; swopusa.org

Sexual Health Counseling and Referral Hotline (Planned Parenthood). *Information and support on birth control, emergency contraception, pregnancy options, sexually transmitted infections including HIV-AIDS, and other aspects of reproductive health.* 800-258-4448 option 4 / 617-616-1616; plannedparenthood.org/online-tools/chat

StrongHearts Native Helpline. *Resources for Native American and Alaska Native people experiencing abuse.* 844-762-8483; strongheartshelpline.org

Tahirih Justice Center. *Free legal and social services to immigrants experiencing gender-based violence, including forced marriage, trafficking, and genital mutilation.* 410-999-1900 / 571-282-6161; tahirih.org

Therapy for Black Girls. *A directory of therapists, wellness resources, and a podcast for Black women and girls.* therapyforblackgirls.com

Therapy for Latinx. *Resources and education for Latinx people seeking mental health services.* therapyforlatinx.com

Therapy for Muslims. *Resources and education for Muslims seeking mental health services.* therapyformuslims.com

Trans Lifeline. *A peer support hotline by and for trans people that's divested from police.* 877-565-8860; translifeline.org; translifeline.org/resource/self-care-emotional -support

TransformHarm.org. *Articles and other resources dedicated to ending violence through a transformative justice, abolitionist lens.* transformharm.org

The Trevor Project. *A 24-7 hotline, text, and chat service and educational resources for LGBTQIA+ youth.* 866-488-7386; thetrevorproject.org

ADVICE COLUMNISTS WHO ARE GREAT AT BOUNDARIES

Carolyn Hax. washingtonpost.com/people/carolyn-hax

Jennifer Peepas, Captain Awkward: Advice and Commiseration. captainawkward.com

Kai Cheng Thom, Ask Kai: Advice for the Apocalypse. xtramagazine.com/series /ask-kai-advice-for-the-apocalypse

Sahaj Kaur Kohli, Ask Sahaj. washingtonpost.com/people/sahaj-kaur-kohli

BOOKS AND ARTICLES WE LOVE

Babcock, Linda, and Sara Laschever. *Women Don't Ask: The High Cost of Avoiding Negotiation—and Positive Strategies for Change.* New York: Bantam, 2007.

Bates, Laura. *Girl Up: Kick Ass, Claim Your Woman Card, and Crush Everyday Sexism.* New York: Touchstone, 2016.

Bennett, Jessica. *Feminist Fight Club: An Office Survival Manual for a Sexist Workplace.* New York: HarperCollins, 2016.

Black Youth Project 100 (BYP100). Black Queer Feminist Curriculum Toolkit. communityresourcehub.org/resources/she-safe-we-safe-black-queer-feminist -curriculum-toolkit.

Brach, Tara. *Radical Acceptance: Embracing Your Life with the Heart of a Buddha.* New York: Random House, 2004.

brown, adrienne maree. *Emergent Strategy: Shaping Change, Changing Worlds.* Chico, CA: AK Press, 2017.

brown, adrienne maree. *Pleasure Activism: The Politics of Feeling Good.* Chico, CA: AK Press, 2019.

de Becker, Gavin. *The Gift of Fear: And Other Survival Signals That Protect Us from Violence.* New York: Little, Brown, 1997.

Chemaly, Soraya. *Rage Becomes Her: The Power of Women's Anger.* New York: Atria Books, 2018.

Chen, Ching-In, Jai Dulani, and Leah Lakshmi Piepzna-Samarasinha. *The Revolution Starts at Home: Confronting Partner Abuse in Activist Communities.* Chico, CA: AK Press, 2016. criticalresistance.org/wp-content/uploads/2014/05/Revolution-starts-at-home-zine.pdf.

Cooper, Brittney. *Eloquent Rage: A Black Feminist Discovers Her Superpower.* New York: Picador, 2019.

Creative Interventions Tool Kit: A Practical Guide to Stop Interpersonal Violence. creative -interventions.org/toolkit.

Davis, Angela, Gina Dent, Erica R. Meiners, and Beth E. Richie. *Abolition. Feminism. Now.* Chicago: Haymarket Books, 2021.

DiAngelo, Robin. *White Fragility: Why It's So Hard for White People to Talk about Racism.* Boston: Beacon Press, 2018.

Dixon, Ejeris, and Leah Lakshmi Piepzna-Samarasinha. *Beyond Survival: Strategies and Stories from the Transformative Justice Movement.* Chico, CA: AK Press, 2020.

Eltahawy, Mona. *The Seven Necessary Sins for Women and Girls.* Boston: Beacon Press, 2020.

Febos, Melissa. "I Spent My Life Consenting to Touch I Didn't Want." *New York Times Magazine,* March 31, 2021. nytimes.com/2021/03/31/magazine/consent.html.

Flaherty, Jordan. *No More Heroes: Grassroots Challenges to the Savior Mentality.* Chico, CA: AK Press, 2016.

Friedman, Jaclyn, and Jessica Valenti. *Yes Means Yes: Visions of Female Sexual Power and a World without Rape.* Berkeley, CA: Seal Press, 2008.

Gay, Roxane. *Not That Bad: Dispatches from Rape Culture.* New York: Harper Perennial, 2018.

Girls for Gender Equity, Inc., Joanne N. Smith, Mandy Van Deven, and Meghan Huppuch. *Hey Shorty! A Guide to Combating Sexual Harassment and Violence in Schools and on the Streets.* New York: Feminist Press, 2011.

Haga, Kazu. *Healing Resistance: A Radically Different Response to Harm.* Berkeley, CA: Parallax Press, 2020.

Haines, Staci K. *The Politics of Trauma: Somatics, Healing, and Social Justice.* Berkeley, CA: North Atlantic Books, 2019.

Haines, Staci K. *The Survivor's Guide to Sex: How to Have an Empowered Sex Life After Child Sexual Abuse.* San Francisco: Cleis Press, 1999.

Hall, Marcia E. *Lifelines: Women, Male Violence, and Personal Safety.* Baltimore: PublishAmerica, 2003.

Harper, Faith G. *Unf*ck Your Brain: Using Science to Get Over Anxiety, Depression, Anger, Freak-Outs, and Triggers.* Portland, OR: Microcosm Publishing, 2017.

Herman, Judith Lewis. *Trauma and Recovery: The Aftermath of Violence—from Domestic Abuse to Political Terror.* New York: Basic Books, 2015.

Hopper, James W. "Why Many Rape Victims Don't Fight or Yell." *Washington Post,* June 23, 2015. washingtonpost.com/news/grade-point/wp/2015/06/23/why-many-rape -victims-dont-fight-or-yell.

INCITE! Women of Color Against Violence. *Color of Violence: The INCITE! Anthology.* Cambridge, MA: South End Press, 2006.

Irving, Debby. *Waking Up White: And Finding Myself in the Story of Race.* Cambridge, MA: Elephant Room Press, 2014.

Kaba, Mariame, and the Chicago Alliance to Free Marissa Alexander, eds. *No Selves to Defend: A Legacy of Criminalizing Women of Color for Self-Defense.* noselves2defend.files .wordpress.com/2016/09/noselvestodefend_v5.pdf.

Kaba, Mariame. *We Do This 'Til We Free Us: Abolitionist Organizing and Transforming Justice.* Chicago: Haymarket Books, 2021.

Kendi, Ibram X. *How to Be an Antiracist.* New York: One World, 2019.

King, Ruth. *Healing Rage: Women Making Inner Peace Possible.* New York: Avery, 2008.

Leung, Debbie. *Self-Defense: The Womanly Art of Self-Care, Intuition, and Choice.* Tacoma, WA: R & M Press, 1991. Out-of-print book available from the author at PO Box 1153, Olympia, WA 98507.

Levine, Peter A. *Waking the Tiger: Healing Trauma.* Berkeley, CA: North Atlantic Books, 1997.

Maltz, Wendy. *The Sexual Healing Journey: A Guide for Survivors of Sexual Abuse.* New York: William Morrow, 2012.

Mattingly, Katy. *Self-Defense: Steps to Survival.* Champaign, IL: Human Kinetics, 2007.

McCaughey, Martha. *Real Knockouts: The Physical Feminism of Women's Self-Defense.* New York: New York University Press, 1997.

McKeown, Greg. "If You Don't Prioritize Your Own Life, Someone Else Will." *Harvard Business Review*, June 28, 2012. hbr.org/2012/06/how-to-say-no-to-a-controlling.

Menakem, Resmaa. *My Grandmother's Hands: Racialized Trauma and the Pathway to Mending Our Hearts and Bodies.* Las Vegas, NV: Central Recovery Press, 2017.

Mighty Forces, Southpaw Insights, Upstream Analysis, and Grey Horse Communications. *The Self-Promotion Gap: Exploring Women's Resistance to Self-Promotion.* selfpromotiongap .com/home.

Mogul, Joey L., Andrea J. Ritchie, and Kay Whitlock. *Queer (In)Justice: The Criminalization of LGBT People in the United States.* Boston: Beacon Press, 2012.

Nagoski, Emily. *Come as You Are: The Surprising New Science That Will Transform Your Sex Life.* New York: Simon & Schuster, 2021.

Neff, Kristin. *Fierce Self-Compassion: How Women Can Harness Kindness to Speak Up, Claim Their Power, and Thrive.* New York: Harper Wave, 2021.

Oluo, Ijeoma. *So You Want to Talk about Race.* New York: Seal Press, 2018.

Owens, Lama Rod. *Love and Rage: The Path of Liberation through Anger.* Berkeley, CA: North Atlantic Books, 2020.

Ortner, Nick. *The Tapping Solution: A Revolutionary System for Stress-Free Living.* Carlsbad, CA: Hay House, 2013.

Piepzna-Samarasinha, Leah Lakshmi. *Care Work: Dreaming Disability Justice.* Vancouver, BC: Arsenal Pulp Press, 2018.

Ritchie, Andrea J. *Invisible No More: Police Violence against Black Women and Women of Color.* Boston: Beacon Press, 2017.

Saad, Layla F. *Me and White Supremacy: Combat Racism, Change the World, and Become a Good Ancestor.* Naperville, IL: Sourcebooks, 2020.

Schenwar, Maya, Joe Macaré, and Alana Yu-lan Price, eds. *Who Do You Serve, Who Do You Protect? Police Violence and Resistance in the United States.* Chicago: Haymarket Books, 2016.

Schwartz, Arielle. *The Complex PTSD Workbook.* Berkeley, CA: Althea Press, 2017.

Simmons, Aishah Shahidah. *Love WITH Accountability: Digging Up the Roots of Child Sexual Abuse.* Chico, CA: AK Press, 2019.

Sins Invalid. *Skin, Tooth, and Bone: The Basis of Movement Is Our People.* sinsinvalid.org /disability-justice-primer.

Snortland, Ellen. *Beauty Bites Beast: Awakening the Warrior within Women and Girls.* Pasadena, CA: Trilogy Books, 1998.

Taket, Anne, and Beth R. Crisp. *Eliminating Gender-Based Violence.* New York: Routledge, 2018.

Tawwab, Nedra Glover. *Set Boundaries, Find Peace: A Guide to Reclaiming Yourself.* New York: TarcherPerigee, 2021.

Taylor, Lauren R. "What to Say—and What Not to Say—When Someone Tells You They Have Been Sexually Assaulted." *Lily,* September 25, 2018. thelily.com/what-to-say-and -what-not-to-say-when-someone-tells-you-they-have-been-sexually-assaulted.

Taylor, Sonya Renee. *The Body Is Not an Apology: The Power of Radical Self-Love.* Oakland, CA: Berrett-Koehler Publishers, 2021.

Traister, Rebecca. *Good and Mad: The Revolutionary Power of Women's Anger.* New York: Simon & Schuster, 2018.

Ury, William. *The Power of a Positive No: Save the Deal, Save the Relationship—and Still Say No.* New York: Bantam, 2007.

van der Kolk, Bessel. *The Body Keeps the Score: Brain, Mind, and Body in the Healing of Trauma.* New York: Penguin Books, 2015.

Wanamaker, Lynne Marie, et al. *Say Something Superhero Field Guide: A Manual for Eliminating Interpersonal Violence.* safepass.org/wp-content/uploads/2018/09/SS -FieldGuide-2015.pdf.

Wiest, Brianna. "This Is What 'Self-Care' REALLY Means, Because It's Not All Salt Baths and Chocolate Cake." *Thought Catalog*, May 17, 2022. thoughtcatalog.com /brianna-wiest/2017/11/this-is-what-self-care-really-means-because-its-not-all-salt -baths-and-chocolate-cake.

williams, Rev. angel Kyodo, Lama Rod Owens, and Jasmine Syedullah. *Radical Dharma: Talking Race, Love, and Liberation.* Berkeley, CA: North Atlantic Books, 2016.

Wong, Kristin. "Dealing with Imposter Syndrome When You're Treated as an Imposter." *New York Times,* June 12, 2018. nytimes.com/2018/06/12/smarter-living/dealing-with -impostor-syndrome-when-youre-treated-as-an-impostor.html.

PODCASTS AND VIDEOS

Bernstein, Rachel. *IndoctriNation.* Podcast. rachelbernsteintherapy.com/podcast.html.

Brown, Autumn, and adrienne maree brown. *How to Survive the End of the World.* Podcast. endoftheworldshow.org.

Cuddy, Amy. "Your Body Language May Shape Who You Are." TED, 2012. Video, 20:46. ted.com/talks/amy_cuddy_your_body_language_may_shape_who_you_are.

Hemphill, Prentis. *Finding Our Way with Prentis Hemphill.* Podcast. findingourwaypodcast.com.

L'Oréal Paris USA. "Lessons of Worth with Viola Davis." YouTube, May 28, 2020. Video, 2:01. youtube.com/watch?v=GAP2W8g533k.

Martin, Betty. "The Wheel of Consent." Videos. bettymartin.org/videos.

Michigan Public Radio. *Believed.* Podcast. believed.michiganradio.org.

Solarte-Erlacher, Marisol. *Resilience and Resistance.* Podcast. marisolerlacher.com/podcast.

Vernacchio, Al. "Sex Needs a New Metaphor: Here's One . . ." TED, July 15, 2013. Video, 8:21. youtube.com/watch?v=xF-CX9mAHPo.

GET INVOLVED

A Call to Men. *Offering trainings and resources to help create a world where all men and boys are loving and respectful and all women, girls, and those at the margins are valued and safe.* acalltomen.org

The Catcall Collective. *A place to share stories of gender-based violence.* instagram .com/thecatcallcollective

The Community Resource Hub for Safety and Accountability. *Resources on transformative and restorative justice, police sexual assault, alternatives to policing, conflict resolution, and more.* communityresourcehub.org/resources

Creative Interventions. *A community accountability and transformative justice organization providing education and resources on community-based, non-carceral responses to violence.* creative-interventions.org/actions

End Abuse of People with Disabilities (Vera Institute of Justice). *A project activating people and organizations to end violence against people with disabilities and D/deaf people; includes resources under Tools and Training.* endabusepwd.org

FreeFrom. *A queer-, trans-, immigrant-, and BIPOC-led organization supporting survivors' collective economic and community power through building survivors' wealth and financial security.* freefrom.org

The HEAL Project. *A QTBIPOC-, disabled-, and survivor-led educational initiative using media to prevent and end childhood sexual abuse through healing the wounds of sexual oppression and embracing sexual liberation.* heal2end.org/home

Healing Histories Project. *A healing justice organization cataloging medical violence, harms, and abuses rooted in racism and capitalism and engaging individuals, communities, and institutions to remember these abuses and harms by catalyzing research, action, and movement-building strategies.* healinghistoriesproject.com

Interrupting Criminalization. *An organization aiming to interrupt and end the criminalization and incarceration of women, girls, trans, and gender-nonconforming people of color for acts related to public order, poverty, child welfare, drug use, survival, and self-defense, including criminalization and incarceration of survivors of violence.* interruptingcriminalization.com

Men Can Stop Rape (MCSR). *An organization mobilizing men to create violence-free cultures through healthy masculinity trainings and programming.* mcsr.org

Mentors in Violence Prevention (MVP). *An organization providing mixed-gender, multiracial sexual harassment and gender-violence prevention trainings.* mvpstrat.com

The Nap Ministry. *A wellness organization centering rest as a form of resistance.* thenapministry.wordpress.com

A National Agenda for Black Girls. *A movement-building collaborative project amplifying the needs and voices of Black girls in national policy.* natagenda4blackgirls.org

No Selves to Defend. *A resource hub (check out the Resources tab) supporting survivors of violence who are criminalized for self-defense and survival. Includes an anthology on the legacy of criminalizing women of color for self-defense.* noselves2defend.wordpress.com

Survived and Punished. *An abolitionist organization with advocacy, programming, and resources for criminalized survivors.* survivedandpunished.org

We R Native. *A comprehensive health resource by and for Indigenous youth that includes info on abuse, other violence, healthy relationships, and more.* wernative.org

ACKNOWLEDGMENTS

This book began in the 1970s, when I started karate and my sensei, Gerald Orange, taught me to believe in myself, something foreign to me at the time. He encouraged my teaching of women when that was a rarity. I am forever grateful.

Self Defense from the Inside Out, as it was first titled, grew out of my teaching experiences with Annie Ellman at Brooklyn Women's Martial Arts (now the Center for Anti-Violence Education). Annie's work to empower women, and members of all marginalized groups, has remained a constant inspiration. Our teaching emerged within a larger antiracist movement to address sexual violence and create a more just, respectful, and caring world. I am indebted to leaders in the movements for racial and gender equity and disability rights, whose intersectional analysis expanded my understanding. Too numerous to name, among these influences were the Combahee River Collective, Mobility International, Santa Cruz Women Against Rape, Wendi Dragonfire, Sunny Graff, Marcia Hall, Debbie Leung, and Joan Nelson. We found validation in the groundbreaking research of Pauline Bart, Jennie McIntyre, Patricia O'Brien, and Queen's Bench Foundation, among others, who challenged misinformation and defied fear-based prescriptions for safety that restricted the lives of women and others targeted by violence.

By the late 1980s I was working with Rape Crisis Network in Eugene, Oregon, where Gail Wiemann provided the impetus to create this book. It became a community project, benefiting from assistance in many forms, including format innovations by Rakar West and Lina Van Brunt. Perry Downes facilitated my creation of a course based on the book that reached hundreds of participants through a statewide agency. Over the course of two decades, countless students from New York City, Uganda, Mongolia, Siberia, and Japan, and especially the University of Oregon, further shaped this book through their generous feedback and the courage, honesty, and self-love they brought to the content. They hold a special place in my heart.

In 2003 I embarked on a revision, encouraged by those who had found the earlier version life changing and insisted that I get it out into the world. This phase was supported by the generous review of many colleagues, including Phyllis Barkhurst, Elly Maloney, Beth Monterrosa, Bay Ostrach, Ellen Rifkin, tova Stabin, Peg Strain, and participants in workshops hosted by the National Women's Martial Arts Federation (NWMAF) and Pacific Association of Women Martial Artists.

While the book circulated through community networks, it was never formally published. When a health crisis took me to Maryland, a silver lining appeared in the form of my colleague Lauren R. Taylor. Lauren agreed to take up this current version, applying her writing and logistical skills, securing both agent and publisher, and doing the lion's share of revisions. I am grateful to Lauren beyond words. Together we thank our agent, Elaine Spencer, and our editors, Lauren Appleton and Ashley Alliano, for believing in us and doing everything necessary to place the book into your hands.

Marcia Hall, Aloha Heart, Ashanti Li, Carter McKenzie, Lisa Ponder, Ellen Rifkin, Oblio Stroyman, Jen Swinehart, and Susan Sygall all contributed their wisdom to this final version. Our self-defense research guru, Jocelyn Hollander, generously answered questions and helped us think through challenging areas. This book also reflects the pioneering self-defense work of the Center for Anti-Violence Education, NWMAF's Nancy Lanoue, Marie O'Brien, Jaye Spiro, Martha Thompson, and my coauthor, Lauren; Yehudit Zicklin-Sidikman and all who have developed empowerment self-defense (ESD) into a global movement; and everyone who has participated in the movement to end gender-based violence.

My deep gratitude to those unnamed here due to restrictions of space and memory and to my parents, who gave me the freedom to pursue my dreams.

ACKNOWLEDGMENTS

My spouse, Diane DePaolis, is my rock. She has supported me over the years, bolstered me with encouragement, and patiently endured my disappearing act as I worked on this manuscript for hours on end.

When I started this work we were a small band met with skepticism and even derision. The roots of this work are now wide and deep, fed and watered by every member of a targeted or marginalized group who tapped into their power from the inside out. I finish this final version of *Get Empowered* inspired by *you*—reader-participants, teachers, martial artists, organizers, and activists who are seeing, and acting on, what is needed today and for generations into the future.

—Nadia Telsey, 2023

This book really did take a village—a big village!

My greatest gratitude goes to everyone brave enough, scared enough, or both, to ever come through the doors of a Defend Yourself class. In reclaiming your lives, you are the greatest teachers.

Thank you to Nadia Telsey, for graciously inviting me into this huge and gratifying project with her.

Enormous appreciation and admiration for all Defend Yourself's and Safe Bars's team members and supporters since the beginning. You're incredibly dedicated and skilled, and I count myself very fortunate to have collaborated with each one of you.

I'm deeply thankful to everyone who read the full manuscript and shared their thoughtful, honest feedback: Aya Laurel Iwai-Folk, Carrie Slack, Chaitra Shenoy, Ishita Bal, Juno Baker (Writing Diversely), Kaisa Nichols-Russell, Lynn Brown (Literary Lynn), Lynne Marie Wanamaker, Querube Suárez Jaén, Rita Sengupta, Simone Van Taylor, and Taylor Thompson.

A deep bow to all the foremothers of empowerment self-defense, including my first teacher, Carol Middleton, and to all my colleagues and partners in making "good trouble," especially those in the Empowerment Self-Defense Alliance, my work and passion home. Also to everyone I've ever learned from and trained with.

I honor Minal Hajratwala, the team at the Unicorn Authors Club, and the many unicorns with whom I wrote and groaned and problem-solved and lifted up and celebrated.

Huge credit to those who stepped in with practical help when things were getting dicey: Katy Mattingly, Kerry Kilburn, Nita Apple, and Sahim Lalani.

I want to acknowledge the entire Penguin Random House team for their passion and commitment to this book, including editors Lauren Appleton and Ashley Alliano; our agent, Elaine Spencer at The Knight Agency; and our brilliant and patient illustrator, Nadia Fisher, and her agent, Jemiscoe Chambers-Black at the Andrea Brown Literary Agency.

I'm also grateful to everyone who answered a question, gave an opinion, sat and wrote with me, encouraged me, contributed content, and more: Alena Schaim, Alex Kapitan (the Radical Copyeditor), Anne Kuzminsky, Anthony Amorcito, Carrie Slack, Charlie Gilkey and Angela Wheeler (Productive Flourishing), Crystal Middlestadt, Diane Long, David Van Taylor, Evelyn Torton Beck, Farah Fossé, Heather Ratcliff, Jaime Grant, Jan Parker, Jen Resnick, Jocelyn Hollander, Katherine Ortiz, Katy Mattingly, Keisha Derricott-Bailey, Laura Hutchinson (thanks for the puppy story), Laura Nichols, Lauren McEwen, Loree Cook-Daniels, Lyn Stoesen, Martha Thompson, Macy Freeman, Meg Stone, Nancy Polikoff, Nasreen Alkhateeb, Natalie Miller, Raesin Caine, Risa Shaw, Rita Sengupta (big mwah! for lots of help on the book proposal), Sarah Trembath, Shanda Poitra, Susan Schorn, Tamara Gallman, Taylor Nunley, Teo Drake, and Yuko Uchikawa. I'm sure I've left out some people; please know I appreciate your contributions too.

To the Free Rads (Beth Grupp, Brigette Rouson, Heather Berthoud, Lisa Silverberg, and Lucía Perillán), and to La Sarmiento (my teacher-friend) and the members of Cloud Sangha: I can't tell you how much it means to me that you were with me on this journey. Thanks to all my near and dear ones who kept me afloat with food and hugs and more.

Last but very much not least, to Elizabeth Sternberg, who for the past six years has made everything possible. Thank you.

—Lauren R. Taylor, 2023

NOTES

WELCOME

viii.   ***"Boundaries are the distance"***: Prentis Hemphill (@prentishemphill), "Forgiveness is not for everyone," Instagram, May 6, 2019, instagram.com/p /BxIX1T2A7hr.

xvii.   ***The Self-Defense Paradox:*** Lynne Marie Wanamaker, "Prevention, Resistance, Recovery, Revolution: Feminist Empowerment Self-Defence," in *Eliminating Gender Based Violence*, ed. Ann Taket and Beth R. Crisp (London: Routledge, 2017).

CHAPTER 1: WHERE YOU'RE GOING

9.   ***"Caring for myself"***: Audre Lorde, *A Burst of Light and Other Essays* (Mineola, NY: Ixia Press, 2017).

CHAPTER 2: MORE THAN RAPE

18.   ***The more marginalized identities a person:*** "Sexual Assault," VAWnet, accessed July 6, 2022, vawnet.org/sc/gender-based-violence-and-intersecting -challenges-impacting-native-american-alaskan-village-1.

18.   ***for example, Indigenous:*** Stéphanie Wahab and Lenora Olson, "Intimate Partner Violence and Sexual Assault in Native American Communities," *Trauma, Violence & Abuse: A Review Journal* 5, no. 4 (2004): 353–66.

18.   ***women, bisexual women:*** Reina Gattuso, "Why Bisexual Women Are at a Higher Risk for Violence," *Teen Vogue*, December 6, 2019, teenvogue.com/story/why -bisexual-women-are-at-a-higher-risk-for-violence; M. L. Walters, J. Chen, and M. J. Breiding, *The National Intimate Partner and Sexual Violence Survey (NISVS):*

2010 Findings on Victimization by Sexual Orientation (Atlanta: National Center for Injury Prevention and Control and Centers for Disease Control and Prevention, 2013), 1, cdc.gov/violenceprevention/pdf/nisvs_sofindings.pdf.

18.   *trans women of color (especially:* Jaime M. Grant et al., *Injustice at Every Turn: A Report of the National Transgender Discrimination Survey* (Washington, DC: National Center for Transgender Equality and National Gay and Lesbian Task Force, 2011), transequality.org/sites/default/files/docs/resources/NTDS _Report.pdf.

18.   *(including intellectual disabilities):* Kathleen C. Basile, Matthew J. Breiding, and Sharon G. Smith, "Disability and Risk of Recent Sexual Violence in the United States," *American Journal of Public Health* 106, no. 5 (2016): 928–33.

21.   *almost 90% of all rapes:* Michele C. Black et al., *National Intimate Partner and Sexual Violence Survey: 2010 Summary Report* (Atlanta: National Center for Injury Prevention and Control and Centers for Disease Control and Prevention, 2011), 21–23, cdc.gov/violenceprevention/pdf/nisvs_report2010-a.pdf.

21.   *Danger lies (in this order):* Black et al., *National Intimate Partner and Sexual Violence Survey: 2010 Summary Report.*

21.   *Two-thirds of sexual violence:* Michael Planty et al., *Female Victims of Sexual Violence, 1994–2010* (Washington, DC: U.S. Department of Justice, Office of Justice Programs, Bureau of Justice Statistics, 2013), 4, bjs.ojp.gov/content /pub/pdf/fvsv9410.pdf.

21.   *Nine out of ten attackers:* Planty et al., *Female Victims of Sexual Violence,* 5.

21.   *More than half of the time:* Rachel E. Morgan, *Race and Hispanic Origin of Victims and Offenders, 2012–15* (Washington, DC: U.S. Department of Justice, Office of Justice Programs, Bureau of Justice Statistics, 2017), 1, bjs.ojp.gov /content/pub/pdf/rhovo1215.pdf.

22.   *much more likely to be a stranger:* André B. Rosay, "Violence against American Indian and Alaska Native Women and Men," *National Institute of Justice Journal* (June 1, 2016), figure 1, nij.ojp.gov/topics/articles/violence-against -american-indian-and-alaska-native-women-and-men; Steven W. Perry, *American Indians and Crime: A BJS Statistical Profile, 1992–2002* (Washington, DC: U.S. Department of Justice, Office of Justice Programs, Bureau of Justice Statistics, 2004), iii, v, 8–10, bjs.ojp.gov/content/pub/pdf/aic02.pdf.

25.   *The myth of the "dangerous Black man":* John Paul Wilson, Kurt Hugenberg, and Nicholas O. Rule, "Racial Bias in Judgments of Physical Size and Formidability: From Size to Threat," *Journal of Personality and Social*

Psychology 113, no. 1 (2017): 59–80, apa.org/pubs/journals/releases/psp-pspi0000092.pdf.

25. *most violence is* intraracial: Rachel E. Morgan and Alexandra Thompson, *Criminal Victimization, 2020—Supplemental Statistical Tables* (Washington, DC: U.S. Department of Justice, Office of Justice Programs, Bureau of Justice Statistics, 2022), table 5, bjs.ojp.gov/content/pub/pdf/cv20sst.pdf.

CHAPTER 3: HOW GENDER-BASED VIOLENCE HAPPENS

34. *for example, trans women of color:* "Sexual Violence & Transgender/Non-Binary Communities," National Sexual Violence Resource Center, accessed July 13, 2022, nsvrc.org/sites/default/files/publications/2019-02/Transgender_infographic_508_0.pdf.

34. *women), bisexual women:* Reina Gattuso, "Why Bisexual Women Are at a Higher Risk for Violence," *Teen Vogue*, December 6, 2019, teenvogue.com/story/why-bisexual-women-are-at-a-higher-risk-for-violence.

34. *Children and young people are also abused:* Sharon G. Smith et al., *The National Intimate Partner and Sexual Violence Survey: 2015 Data Brief—Updated Release* (Atlanta: National Center for Injury Prevention and Control and Centers for Disease Control and Prevention, 2018), figure 3, cdc.gov/violenceprevention/pdf/2015data-brief508.pdf.

36. *Most sexual assault (as well as:* Michael Planty et al., *Female Victims of Sexual Violence* (Washington, DC: U.S. Department of Justice, Office of Justice Programs, Bureau of Justice Statistics, 2016), 4, bjs.ojp.gov/content/pub/pdf/fvsv9410.pdf.

50. *"Imagine you're at a party":* Jennifer Peepas, "The Art of 'No,' Continued: Saying No When You've Already Said Yes," CaptainAwkward.com, March 24, 2011, captainawkward.com/2011/03/24/the-art-of-no-continued-saying-no-when-youve-already-said-yes.

CHAPTER 4: IS THERE SOMETHING WRONG WITH ME?

52. *"Trauma in a person":* Resmaa Menakem, Resmaa Menakem: Embodied Anti-Racist Education, accessed July 13, 2022, resmaa.com.

56. *ability to recover and heal:* Sarah E. Ullman et al., "Structural Models of the Relations of Assault Severity, Social Support, Avoidance Coping, Self-Blame, and PTSD among Sexual Assault Survivors," *Psychology of Women Quarterly* 31, no. 1 (2007): 23–37; Susan E. Borja, Jennifer L. Callahan, and Patricia J.

Long, "Positive and Negative Adjustment and Social Support of Sexual Assault Survivors," *Journal of Traumatic Stress* 19, no. 6 (2006): 905–14.

56.   *women often participate in victim-blaming:* Lyz Lenz, "White Women Vote Republican. Get Used to It, Democrats," *Washington Post*, November 27, 2020, washingtonpost.com/opinions/2020/11/27/white-women-vote-republican-get -used-it-democrats.

56.   *gender-based violence (mostly women:* Michele C. Black et al., *National Intimate Partner and Sexual Violence Survey: 2010 Summary Report* (Atlanta: National Center for Injury Prevention and Control and Centers for Disease Control and Prevention, 2011), 1, cdc.gov/violenceprevention/pdf/nisvs_report2010-a.pdf.

56.   *and LGBTQIA+ people):* M. L. Walters, J. Chen, and M. J. Breiding, *The National Intimate Partner and Sexual Violence Survey (NISVS): 2010 Findings on Victimization by Sexual Orientation* (Atlanta: National Center for Injury Prevention and Control and Centers for Disease Control and Prevention, 2013), 1, cdc.gov/ violenceprevention/pdf/nisvs_sofindings.pdf; Annah K. Bender and Janet L. Lauritsen, "Violent Victimization among Lesbian, Gay, and Bisexual Populations in the United States: Findings from the National Crime Victimization Survey, 2017–2018," *American Journal of Public Health* 111, no. 2 (2021): 318–26, doi.org/10.2105 /AJPH.2020.306017, erratum in *American Journal of Public Health* 111, no. 7: e5.

57.   **American Bar Association Journal:** "House of Delegates Redefines Death, Urges Redefinition of Rape, and Undoes the Houston Amendments," *American Bar Association Journal* 61, no. 4 (1975): 463–73, jstor.org/stable/25727143.

63.   *those who resist sexual assault:* Jocelyn A. Hollander, "Women's Self-Defense and Sexual Assault Resistance: The State of the Field," *Sociology Compass* 12, no. 8 (August 2018), compass.onlinelibrary.wiley.com/doi/abs/10.1111/soc4.12597; "The Evidence-Base," Empowerment Self-Defense Alliance, last modified 2019, empowermentsd.org/evidence-base; Jennifer S. Wong and Samantha Balemba, "The Effect of Victim Resistance on Rape Completion: A Meta-Analysis," *Trauma, Violence & Abuse: A Review Journal* 19, no. 3 (2016): 352–65.

63.   *significantly more injuries:* Jongyeon Tark and Gary Kleck, "Resisting Rape: The Effects of Victim Self-Protection on Rape Completion and Injury," *Violence against Women* 20, no. 3 (2014): 270–92; S. E. Ullman, "Does Offender Violence Escalate When Women Fight Back?," *Journal of Interpersonal Violence* 13 (1998): 179–92.

69.   **Women still do the vast majority:** Megan Brenan, "Women Still Handle Main Household Tasks in U.S.," Gallup, January 29, 2020, news.gallup.com /poll/283979/women-handle-main-household-tasks.aspx; Sandrine Lungumbu and Amelia Butterly, "Coronavirus and Gender: More Chores for Women Set

Back Gains in Equality," BBC News, November 26, 2020, bbc.com/news /world-55016842.

69. *states are pushing:* Justine Jablonska, ed., "Seven Charts That Show COVID-19's Impact on Women's Employment," McKinsey & Company, March 8, 2021, mckinsey.com/featured-insights/diversity-and-inclusion/seven-charts-that-show -covid-19s-impact-on-womens-employment; Patricia Cohen, "Recession with a Difference: Women Face Special Burden," *New York Times*, November 17, 2020, nytimes.com/2020/11/17/business/economy/women-jobs-economy-recession.html.

76. *"Your coping mechanisms":* Tara Brach, heard by Lauren R. Taylor at a dharma talk, year unknown.

CHAPTER 5: FIRST, YOU HAVE TO BELIEVE

88. *"Can you imagine an animal":* Gavin de Becker, *The Gift of Fear: Survival Signals That Protect Us from Violence* (New York: Little, Brown, 1997), 30.

97. *"But eventually, I just got tired":* Michelle Obama, quoted in Maggie Parker, "First Lady Michelle Obama Talks about the Sexism She's Faced," *Time*, March 25, 2016, time.com/4272032/michelle-obama-sexism.

98. *As Juliet Eilperin reported:* Juliet Eilperin, "White House Women Want to Be in the Room Where It Happens," *Washington Post*, September 13, 2016, washingtonpost.com/news/powerpost/wp/2016/09/13/white-house-women -are-now-in-the-room-where-it-happens.

CHAPTER 6: CLAIM YOUR POWER

102. *"You're braver than you believe":* *Pooh's Grand Adventure: The Search for Christopher Robin*, directed by Karl Geurs (Burbank, CA: Walt Disney Home Video, 1997).

103. *Look at the feelings wheel:* Based on work by Gloria Willcox. See Willcox, "The Feeling Wheel: A Tool for Expanding Awareness of Emotions and Increasing Spontaneity and Intimacy," *Transactional Analysis Journal* 12, no. 4 (1982): 274–76, doi.org/10.1177/036215378201200411.

110. *"When you're not used to being":* Vassilia Binensztok (@junocounseling), "When you're not used to being confident, confidence feels like arrogance . . .," Twitter, May 23, 2021, 10:52 a.m., twitter.com/junocounseling/status/1396479203541934086.

117. *article about imposter syndrome:* Rashika Tulshyan and Jodi-Ann Burey, "Stop Telling Women They Have Imposter Syndrome," *Harvard Business Review*,

February 11, 2021, hbr.org/2021/02/stop-telling-women-they-have-imposter -syndrome.

CHAPTER 7: BECOME AN ACTIVE RESISTER

130. *"I think of myself as":* Angela Chen quoted in Nicole Chung, "You Do Not Always Have to Say Yes," *Atlantic*, January 19, 2022, newsletters.theatlantic .com/i-have-notes/61e6dcd93a37470020ccac2d/learning-to-say-no.

141. *"[Self-love is] a decision":* Lizzo, "Self-Care Has to Be Rooted in Self-Preservation, Not Just Mimosas and Spa Days," *Think*, NBC News, April 19, 2019, nbcnews.com/think/opinion/self-care-has-be-rooted-self-preservation -not-just-mimosas-ncna993661.

CHAPTER 8: YOU HAVE CHOICES

158. *Life coach Jamila White:* Jamila White (@InspiredJamila), "Ultra-independence is a trauma response . . .," Instagram, January 14, 2023, instagram.com/p/CFKMmD3hB7j.

160. *First, remember that:* Michele C. Black et al., *National Intimate Partner and Sexual Violence Survey: 2010 Summary Report* (Atlanta: National Center for Injury Prevention and Control and Centers for Disease Control and Prevention, 2011), table 2.5, cdc.gov/violenceprevention/pdf/NISVS_Report2010-a.pdf.

160. *half of all attacks:* Black et al., *National Intimate Partner and Sexual Violence Survey: 2010 Summary Report*, table 2.6.

161. *"I am never proud":* Maya Angelou, "In Self-Defense," in *Letter to My Daughter* (London: Virago, 2014): 101–3.

164. *Weapons are used:* Craig Perkins, "Weapon Use and Violent Crime," *National Crime Victimization Survey, 1993–2001* (Washington, DC: U.S. Department of Justice, Office of Justice Programs, Bureau of Justice Statistics, 2003), 1, bjs .ojp.gov/content/pub/pdf/wuvc01.pdf.

166. *When faced with a threat:* Kasia Kozlowska et al., "Fear and the Defense Cascade: Clinical Implications and Management," *Harvard Review of Psychiatry* 23, no. 4 (2015): 263–87, ncbi.nlm.nih.gov/pmc/articles/PMC4495877.

CHAPTER 9: GET YOUR MESSAGE ACROSS

176. *one-third of what's communicated:* Allen Pease and Barbara Pease, "Understanding the Basics," in *The Definitive Book of Body Language* (Chatswood,

Australia: Harlequin Enterprises, 2017): 7–30, excerpted at nytimes.com /2006/09/24/books/chapters/0924-1st-peas.html.

199. *"this grows out of the taproot"*: Carolyn Hax, "Carolyn Hax Live Chat: My Stepmother-in-Law Is Rude to Me When We're Alone," *Washington Post*, April 30, 2021, washingtonpost.com/lifestyle/2021/04/30/live-chat-carolyn-hax.

CHAPTER 10: WHAT'S NEXT

212. *"Rarely, if ever"*: bell hooks, *All about Love* (New York: William Morrow, 2018), 215.

214. *Even people who* imagined *a friend:* Simone Schnall et al., "Social Support and the Perception of Geographical Slant," *Journal of Experimental Social Psychology* 44, no. 5 (2008): 1246–55, ncbi.nlm.nih.gov/pmc/articles /PMC3291107.

222. *"[Practicing radical self-care] means"*: Angela Davis, "Radical Self-Care," AFROPUNK, December 17, 2018, video, 4:27, youtube.com /watch?v=Q1cHoL4vaBs.

ABOUT EMPOWERMENT SELF-DEFENSE

237. *ESD teaches practical skills:* Jocelyn A. Hollander, "Empowerment Self-Defense Frequently Asked Questions (FAQ)," accessed December 7, 2022, jocelynhollander.com/empowerment-self-defense-frequently-asked -questions-faq.

239. *Several studies have found:* Jocelyn A. Hollander, "Women's Self-Defense and Sexual Assault Resistance: The State of the Field," *Sociology Compass* 12, no. 8 (August 2018), compass.onlinelibrary.wiley.com/doi/abs/10.1111/soc4.12597.

239. *College women in the U.S.:* Jocelyn A. Hollander, "Does Self-Defense Training Prevent Sexual Violence against Women?" *Violence against Women* 20, no. 3 (March 2014): 252–69, doi.org/10.1177/1077801214526046.

239. *College women in Canada:* Charlene Y. Senn et al., "Efficacy of a Sexual Assault Resistance Program for University Women," *New England Journal of Medicine* 372, no. 24 (2015), 2326–35, doi.org/10.1056/NEJMsa1411131.

239. *Teen girls in Kenya:* Jake Sinclair et al., "A Self-Defense Program Reduces the Incidence of Sexual Assault in Kenyan Adolescent Girls," *Journal of Adolescent Health* 53, no. 3 (2013), 374–80, doi.org/10.1016/j.jadohealth.2013.04.008.

239. *Participants in a U.S. community class:* Jocelyn A. Hollander and Jeanine Cunningham, "Empowerment Self-Defense Training in a Community Population," *Psychology of Women Quarterly* 44, no. 2 (2020): 187–202, doi .org/10.1177/0361684319897937.

240. *Indigenous girls in South Dakota:* Katie M. Edwards et al., "Effectiveness of a Sexual Assault Self-Defense Program for American Indian Girls," *Journal of Interpersonal Violence* 37, no. 15–16 (August 2022): NP13245–67, doi.org/10.1177/0886260521997942.

240. *Research also shows that ESD:* Hollander and Cunningham, "Empowerment Self-Defense Training in a Community Population"; Jocelyn A. Hollander, "'I Can Take Care of Myself': The Impact of Self-Defense Training on Women's Lives," *Violence against Women* 10, no. 3 (2004): 205–35, doi.org /10.1177/1077801203256202; Christine A. Gidycz et al., "Concurrent Administration of Sexual Assault Prevention and Risk Reduction Programming: Outcomes for Women," *Violence against Women* 21, no. 6 (June 2015): 780–800, doi.org/10.1177/107780121557657; Charlene Y. Senn et al., "Sexual Assault Resistance Education's Benefits for Survivors of Attempted and Completed Rape," *Women & Therapy* 45, no. 1 (2022): 47–73, doi.org/10.1080 /02703149.2021.1971425.

240. *Although research on ESD:* Lisa Speidel, "Exploring the Intersection of Race and Gender in Self-Defense Training," *Violence against Women* 20, no. 3 (2014): 309–25, doi.org/10.1177/1077801214526049.

240. *Research is needed that includes:* Jocelyn A. Hollander, "Empowerment Self-Defense," in *Sexual Assault Risk Reduction and Resistance: Theory, Research and Practice*, ed. Lindsay M. Orchowski and Christine A. Gidycz (London: Elsevier, 2018), 221–44.

GLOSSARY

243. *Microaggressions are common verbal:* Based on a definition from Derald Wing Sue, *Microaggressions in Everyday Life: Race, Gender, and Sexual Orientation* (Hoboken, NJ: Wiley, 2010).

244. *A trigger is anything that:* Based on a definition from "Chapter 3: Understanding the Impact of Trauma," *Trauma-Informed Care in Behaviorial Health Services*, National Library of Medicine, accessed January 26, 2023, ncbi.nlm.nih.gov/books/NBK207191.

ABOUT THE AUTHORS

Nadia Telsey and Lauren R. Taylor are pioneers of the field of empowerment self-defense. Both are survivors of gender-based violence who, for a combined seventy-plus years, have been teaching skills for stopping harassment, abuse, and assault of those most often targeted: women, LGBTQIA+ people, teens, children, and disabled people.

Nadia Telsey (she, her, hers) cofounded a feminist martial arts and self-defense school (now the Center for Anti-Violence Education) in Brooklyn, New York, in 1970. She's taught self-defense to thousands of students, including teaching for seventeen years at the University of Oregon, where her class has been the subject of research on the efficacy of the approach. Her work against gender-based violence included many years serving on the Oregon Attorney General's Sexual Assault Task Force and has influenced generations of self-defense instructors both in the United States and around the world.

Photograph by Annie Popkin

Lauren R. Taylor (she/they) has been working to end gender-based violence since 1978, when she cofounded Washington, DC's first shelter for abused women and their children. As a trainer and director of Defend Yourself, she, along with her team, has reached more than forty thousand people in the DC area and nationally. Taylor's work has been featured in *The Washington Post*,

Photograph by Nasreen Alkhateeb

Self, *HuffPost*, and on National Public Radio, *Upworthy*, *Quartz*, Mic, and more. Her writing on interpersonal violence and violence prevention has been widely published in *The Washington Post*, *Everyday Feminism*, the *Ms. Blog*, and other media.